*ms*

*and*

*mirrors*

# ALARMS
## and
## *mirrors*

= by
# ADAM ATKIN

*SEA TREE PRESS*

*New York*

To Pearl

and in memory of my mother Deborah

---

Sea Tree Press
New York

Publisher's Cataloging-in-Publication Data

Atkin, Adam 1926-
Alarms and Mirrors / Adam Atkin

1. Poetry. 2. Title.

811'.5'4     91-67356

ISBN 0-9631360-3-8

Printed in the United States of America

# CONTENTS

# 7. Making / Maker

# 8. Soundings and Endings

# 9. Into Light

# PREFACE

... We go out to meet the world not only by way of
expediency but also by the way of wonder. In the first we
accumulate information in order to dominate; in the
second we deepen our appreciation in order to respond.
Power is the language of expediency; poetry the
language of wonder. ... Mankind will not perish for want
of information, but only for want of appreciation. ...

> [Heschel, AJ, 1951 (*Man Is Not
> Alone*), pp. 36-7.]

**Who --**

Children are open to the world, and curious. My early
curiosities were not squelched -- at least not entirely. I was
seriously trying to unravel the fantastically contradictory worlds I
experienced -- trying to get a clue to "what's this all about?
Where am I? How can I understand all the craziness around me?
Can violence ever end?" Children asked these questions. I hope
most still do.

My mother was a painter and writer, my father a psychoanalyst.
From an early age, *seeing* interested me deeply, as also did the
structure and dynamics of mind and emotions. When I came to a
dividing of roads, I chose a career in science rather than art. I
went into life sciences, finally into neurophysiology, studying
perception.

**When --**

The earliest of my poems that I can now find date back about
33 years, but I know I wrote a few before that. How did I start to
write poems? Why did I want to? What was I trying to
accomplish?

I remember:

> I wanted to read something that would raise my spirits,
> lighten my spirit -- but I couldn't find anything, so I had
> to try to write it...

> I wanted the intense colorings and rhythms, the high
> warmth of sun coming through stained-glass windows...

Dance, rhythm, blood-pulsation were my life singing to me, asking me to know my life better: therefore I celebrated them...

**What --**

When I write a poem I am amazed each time at what comes together -- the flow of images, words and rhythms, which I guide but do not, in any usual way, "make". Over many years, I have not yet grown accustomed to this -- though I have grown more confident that I can produce the conditions which will allow it to occur, and that when it does, something which I will find of value will be the result. So what is happening? Of course, I don't know.

To intercept the allusions that are submerged in perceptibilities, the interstitial values that never rise to the surface, the indefinable dimension of all existence, is the venture of true poetry.

[Heschel, AJ, 1951 (*Man Is Not Alone*), p. 37.]

Does writing -- and then reading -- poetry give me access to states of awareness, to subtleties of perception, beyond my ordinary habitation? Writing does seem to be an accessing movement -- and the "success" of the poem is the renewal of access afterwards, by reading. Here is what I am implicitly asking: When I read, do I experience a shift of inner state? Do I become more willing (at least for a bit) to *just watch, just listen* -- and to "just feel"? Has the reading thereby enlivened something within me? Does my consciousness become quieter, deeper -- with meaning beyond words glimpsed just beyond the range of my sharp sight? Such *shifts in inner state* are the object. Multiple *resonances* are the object.

Does reading the poem do this? A strong poem evokes simultaneous streams of word-rhythms and of rhythmical transformations of images; these two interlocked and mutually augmenting rhythms engage my whole psyche, pulling thought and feeling into a single complex dance. The poem should somehow pull me out of my seat, an insistent invitation to join its dance. If it does not so *pull* me in, it is not a poem *for me.*

Scientific research has been another interest: Is this part of my life anything like science? Yes and no! In both, I am engaged in exploration and constructive discovery -- am wandering in unknown territories. And in neither do I know all about the countryside in which I hunt, nor can I exactly predetermine my quarry.

More even than the trail of a research enterprise, my writing of poems is always exploration. I drop the hook into the water, without much idea of what will bite. I drag the seine along the hidden bottom, expecting only surprises when I reel it in. I stand very still in the forest, hoping some interesting animals and birds will show themselves -- and they do! Thus I find this writing to be as much a seeking for unknowns as the kinds of scientific research that most intrigued me. The knowledge gained is of a different sort, but no less real or valuable to me.

**Why and How** --

The familiar "I don't know what I think until I hear what I say" seems to have a writer's version that applies strongly to me: I don't know what I understand until I see what I write. What is revealed often points toward unimagined plenitudes, and I find myself opened to a confluence of inner images and rhythms that I could never have constructed or anticipated "deliberately", through "logical decisions". Some one in me speaks who, most of the time, is not heard -- is asleep, or else, cannot shout loudly enough to be heard over the ceaseless racket of inner associational chatter.

This more subtle and less easily heard level may also be in large part associational -- but not quite in the ordinary way. Are the associational processes which give rise to and are evoked by poetry more complex, more multiply-determined than those of "non-poetic thought"? Maybe that is the main key to the difference: in quieting and relaxing, I also slow down -- shift away from rapid, impulsive thought-transitions, toward more deliberately determined associational transitions. The resulting thought sequences would therefore have additional determinants, and more *kinds* of determinants -- that is, *more dimensions of determination.*

But is association all? Insight, intuitive knowledge, is cited as basis for much of the highest creative accomplishment. I intuit that a very deep associational process will result in "insights" not attainable through shallower associational thinking. However, another difference may be important: that of the relations between thought and feeling, between chains of linked ideas and sequences of feeling-states. During my ordinary life, the relation between these two lives within me is very loose -- often thought and feeling have little to do with each other. In higher states of creativity, this changes: thought and feeling mutually strengthen and guide each other; the two streams unite. The union produces something new -- a flow with energy and subtlety that allow it to enter realms totally unknown to the weak, fragmented streams of my "ordinary" inner life.

A meditative state, an inner quietness, permits this deepening and unification. Also, some usual self-censoring can be suspended, at the same time that an attentive discipline is sustained; this leads into an unusual complex of inner discipline with inner freedom.

Ordinarily, when less "quiet", I can only find discipline without freedom or freedom without discipline. I find some seeming discipline but without freedom when busily judging thought sequences for their *usefulness* (usefulness in solving a problem at hand, in planning a course of action, in understanding an immediate situation), or when automatically noting and categorizing familiar aspects of mys situation to maintain my orientation in it, etc. I find some seeming freedom but without discipline when day-dreaming (spinning a fantasy of fear or pleasure, or commenting idly on the passing scene). But neither a disciplined suspension of untrammeled "play of mind" nor a playful but undisciplined suspension of pragmatic censoring is likely to result in much that is new and interesting, because either way the linkages remain shallow -- fast, but of relatively small dimensionality.

Perhaps, in day-dreaming, feeling and thought will flow together in closer mutual influence. But because of the few dimensions under which the process is controlled, day dreaming ordinarily does not lead to much insight. The discipline of poetry, for me, is a patient attentiveness that watches as each present state unfolds and reveals something deeper, waiting for additional linkages to show themselves -- and that listens quietly for the small voice of that which observes these unfoldings and linkages.

Writing is learning. I learn about myself. I learn to see my life and world in unfamiliar yet meaningful, moving ways. The richness of understandings that I make contact with then is a resource I can sometimes draw upon later, when in my more ordinary state of relative "disconnection": Recall of something I had come upon through writing may lead me back toward the more sensitive state in which I originally had the insight...

**1.**

this moment

when . . .

# THIS PLACE

I am a land lost to myself.
(The will knows no maps within):

There is a back country
where the trees rise and
vines climb them.

There is a shore
where small fish browse in shallows.

Marshes at estuaries teem with crabs
that the herons stalk with utmost intentness

(till their double bills stab
downward).

There are deserts a hare sees:
sand and a hard green weed for feeding
(its seed fine as sand).

Sand has hollows (rocks) the desert hare likes:
Shade and hiding are his Sabbath.

# GRATITUDE

The receiver takes himself
        into his hands'
And offers to the
        giver
Himself.

## SEEKING EDGE

Please Pearl, don't reject the buzz
   of inner movements:  know
      skin's heat, mind's pleasing
         hum and
     sizzle.
  Both draw ripples through
this instant's
   tingle.
      It's wild!  Why not be interested in
   the smooth surface
of NOT knowing?
        (I can't find the fault in this mirror-lake.  It hides
        half my life.)

Line and plane:  Point and line determine
   the orthogonal plane.
     Needle
   stands on the mirror.  My
interest won't thread
   its enormous
eye--
        (A target must have limits, or the point can't
        hit it.)

Watch my fingerlight virtuosity, as I
   weave with my needle; can you detect the instant
     its point pierces
        cotton?
     Why should a torn
   bedsheet reveal
private ticking?
   My mattress
     will again be hidden when
   I've sewn
this gap shut.
        (That which supports me must remain
        invisible.  And the hiding will be hidden.)

Here am I!
   I thread this small
     eye with intensity and trembling.
   I can see miniatures
perfectly.  Nevertheless,
   I don't thread the
limitless eye--
        (I pass through every instant without suspecting.)

# EN ROUTE

My breath flows
deep when I
sing

Mind
flutters idly
a bird of tatters

I wish to abide
here, not wise
nor very well
but attentive

Yes, now is
sufficient
unto the day
and night

I have this sneaky
bird in myself
humming

straying
waylaid, awash
marching through surf

# ETERNITY ALWAYS DISAPPEARING

## I. *Watching the Void*

**Strange!** I stay right *here* forever.  The world whirls by.
I, a fixed mechanism, in permanent flux, cycling
      within limits that have grown, over my long history,
A hair's breadth:

        empty persistence, passing the same point continually.

I'm Ptolemaic.  It all turns round <u>me</u>.  A Copernican existence
is conceivable.  But I can't believe it.  Perhaps God
      really <u>is</u> the center.  An intriguing theory!
<u>My</u> time stands still:

        the point of reference about which all revolves.

      (As in the beginning I continue without movement --
          nothing exists for me.  Flashes of sight recur:
          Each lightning-flash finds a rich picture-palace.
    This bright scene grabs and shakes me.  Dust rises, blows away.
    Nothing changes.  Nothing is -- forever.)

**Was** that, then the same as this, now?  I cannot know.
What I have brought with me is <u>here</u>, a few
      souvenirs:  All the rest, vanished forever.
I, the watcher, vanish incessantly, yet

        continually recreate time, tension, torque.

Each second breaks off.  The abyss waits, has no place,
no beginning, no end.  Nothingness is the one solid
      reality.  I am supported by the void.
I dance toward Nirvana:

        this too will pass.  Past emptiness persisting, forever...

## II.  *A Second Shot*


**Sala**! I cycle, turn, *return*. My garden flowering, mouldering.
I watch the invisible movement of myriad growth centers
        from which this green tapestry creates itself.
I breath the self-generation of

                this seamless web, within which I walk, looking out at God.

The center is *so  deep*! I rest within it. Nothing comes between
portrayal and existence. Womb and world are one. Perhaps this
        chapter is the whole story. Nevertheless, I read on!
Histories of histories of histories:

                those who begot indebted forever to the begotten.


        (The path is narrow -- blades flash, water ripples
            far below. This instant persists to eternity.
            Walking along the blade is a blast!
        Joy rips through flesh, a laser knife opening minute channels.
        It's all heaven! It's very hard. It's <u>here</u>.)


**This** time I will hang on! It's hard not dozing.
I dream I awake; my snoring shakes you who walk with me.
        Is this butterfly a philosopher? Hardly likely!
Swimming through air -- easier than staying steady:

                I flutter and falter. I lose the path and plunge.

Each second breaks off. The abyss waits, has no place,
no beginning, no end. Nothingness is the one solid
        reality. I am supported by the void.
I dance toward Nirvana:

                this too will pass. Past emptiness persisting, forever...

# AFOOT

## (chasm, hidden, home)

### I.

I will not sense the danger, grandeur of
    the hidden drop-off.
        Fooled by fog, I speed ahead.

Now the mist lifts: I see gaps, chasms, open waters. Vast tumult
stretches to infinity. Blast and shadow sweep along, hurtling,
hissing... The beach now is not a haven.

When my vision clears and I <u>see</u>
    the abyss I walk beside,
        I am not unhappy.

### II.

*I carry the void, closed*
    *within a crystalline box, there*
*to admire when, in a quiet hour, I can*
    *lift the top and touch it.*

*Jewel beyond price, it means*
    *nothing -- sings no tune, says*
*no verse -- but rests softly, showing*
    *in silence that I exist.*

*This is a gift that I hold*
    *for an instant, then close*
*within its box again. It is <u>there</u>:*
    *Here I am! That place*

        remains
            silent.
        (I keep it
            hidden.)

# RECALL

Harmony
   is to be
   found
Everywhere!
Look:
      concertos of
      crepuscular
Conformation, infinite
Levels of
      pattern nestled one
      within another.


                    *


            How can I


        not
      Marvel?  Why do I
         forget to
Look?
      This rhythm that
               penetrates my
Flesh has
         no
      Respect for
Limits: I
            am a strand
      Woven   into the
            universal


            tapestry.


                    *


9

# INTENSITIES

"What a fantastic panorama!"
"What a succulent, wide-open massage!"

Go easy!
     slide --
     pour into
the overflowing pot:

     *Seeing* is not seen (but burns).
     *Feeling* is not felt (but soars).

       *      *      *

That's how it was yesterday.  That's easy.
In fact, it's <u>nice</u>!  But **now** it's too hot --

Being seared on the stove leaves me no alternative:
     I must ask God to **turn off the gas**.  (If God won't
     I'll jump out of the pan helter skelter,
and take the consequences.)

       *      *      *

Now, baby --
     Calmness,
     Calmness will cure the pain.
     Don't just go for broke!  Go for a long, deep line.
     Let it hang there, the weight resting on the bottom
         of the bay.  (A big flat-fish may eye the bait.

Then you'll have a juicy meal!)

## Exploration

Down into the cellar
                Find the inside door:
Descend to sub-cellar and search
                more: Another door.
More stairs down. A catacomb. It's
                dark. Walk
Down the sloping halls, and watch: How
                deep? Is this an
End? Or can lower openings be found? Where
                is the next descent? Will it be
Detectable? Move the held light along the walls, scan it
                over the floor: Is there any more way
Down? Will the light last? Will I ever
                return? Why stop
Now?

## OBSERVERS

(Breathe.)
See fish
    dart between rocks.

    Watch
        flickering patterns:
        Refracted
    shadows freckle
        pool's bottom.
        (Breathe again.)
    Stand.

    Fish hovers, watching:
gills reciprocate.
(I am seen!)

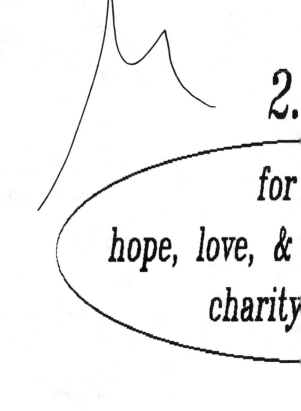

**2.**
for
hope, love, &
charity

# RAKING SONG

/\ /\ /\

Sing each fall
      when leaves flutter
      chilled, then drop
      to mold---

That others in summer
      fell from the limb
Settled as soil or rattled
      drifting from root to root
      to break (bright days)
      to dust on the stones.


And hear:

Children, playing in the yard
      (sky falls hard blue)
      shout lean commands and laugh---

Chaff blasphemies into the shying air
      (where slender sun
      nips leaves down).


\*     \*     \*


Leave heaps lie
Smoldering
Where children---unbrittled

Bright
Watch the burning
Call to each other

Joke
Learn wit (learn
War).

*14*

# RISING

(Prelude to Deluge)


Sad is the day
    In the Spring
        (or in May)

When we walk through the park
    In the sun
        (before dark)

And the Sassafras leaves smell sweet Lemoney-O
And pigeons caroo--to their spouses (near houses)
    While chiggers sip dumbly
    at neat Blood-of-Kine.
Yours and mine.


Flowers bud slowly;
    The sun bleeds
        and drops

Star bells ring gently
    As men count
        their crops

(Hear the wind-woven grain whispering Silvery-O
Of scythes that will turn)--Then the stars turn to rain
    While a thundering train
    whirls my blood, rocks my brain.
Come: The Ark.

## BEFORE SLEEP

### I.

The moment thunders
The pounding is audible.
What is making the incessant sound outside?
I can't hear the engines
But the rocker arm does not stop
(I have asked whether my heart
                    makes these sounds:
It does not.)


Ah---
The marching of thousands (shod) could do it
Are they alive?
The millions that have
Perished are coming back!


(I have taken my pulse and that
                    is not it.
For the noise is a thunder of birds' wings
                    over the Southern pole, beating
                    Against the winds. . . )


But what kind of outrageous fantasy is this?
Of course it is some sort of engine:
It is pumping the water out of graves,
So the dead can be dry.

## II.

Silence
Comes as a lack of
                pressure---
                the lack of
Pushing
Pulls.


I regret that this question remains
(But am already forgetting to ask it:
Now I can hear the distant horns, as
The harbor hints of its existence).


Silence reveals the depths of the spaces beyond
Surrounding walls.
(Sirens wound the grey weather.)


       .     .     .


But:
It has begun again:  strange
                now, after absence,
                slowly recognized.
(It is Icarus flying upward).
I turn out the light.


But remember but remember
                (but remember).
I listen through walls
To footfalls
To pulsing
To pumps
To the fall of wax
                and feathers.


*17*

## TROY

Pine-bough wreathes
Breath slowly

Drying upon the mound.

       Underneath is
       child's

Body
      shattered on rocks
      (at the base

Of the girding wall).

# WAITING

We inhabit a strange, loose world
  shifting so rapidly we can't see the pivots.
  I'm shocked! A thought
Emptied me of concerns and contentions.  It disappeared too.

This planet a dream of butterflies
  waiting for winter.  The next instant,
  life can leak from the universe
Empty forever.

Being is now more finite than ever, as it may
  end in an instant, everywhere.
  This kind of change is too sudden to bear.
I become blind, deaf, dumb,  dead inside, running for my life.

How do the Powerful Men of our Era permit tOTAL tERROR
  to grow unchecked, earth's cancer, needing
  commitments to health beyond the wits of everyone.
To foresee catastrophe is not necessarily to step out of the way.

Are we just waiting?


Do SOMETHING I tell myself and I start to sidle toward an inkling of
what I *might* try to do.
Think of the alternatives.  Hear the cries of babies.  Smell the fragrant
soil.  Wait and listen.  This earth cries out, hardly born and gasping.
Shrieking for life.  "Please don't throw me in the garbage."

We are all together, in pride, in selfishness, in stubbornness.  How
infinitely sad the predicament of the self-righteous.  "Follow the one
True way or be damned forever.  Follow me."   I'm so very sorry.

# COMPILATION

Assembly:
Miracle of light:
   Incandescent particles
   Coalesce into structure, cooling --
Come to life.

This planet:
Being.  Crowd of autocrats:
   How will we restore harmony?
   Was there ever peaceable coexistence
Without wars?

Never:
The harmonious kingdoms are of the minds of men, and God.
   But let's lie down as parents
   And wake up as children, hug and make up;
And sing!

Flow:
Voice scintillates.  I, you, we, they croon
   Each with each, effortless
   Yet paying respectful attention to all sound;
Forever.

It's easy:
I'll just give up the steel walls, barbed wire
   That keep you out.  Who are you?
   It's time we met.  The road will be more pleasant
If we talk.

Hello:
We're coming
   Coming back.  Coming along.
   Coming together --
Assemble!

## A birth-trauma (and yet another one)


You want out?
Good.  Let's leave!
    Too many torments?  The raging dogs bite
    too often?  A desire for peace, a private drifting with the tide?

**OK!  Let's go!  Grab the ring...  <u>Hold on</u>.  We're getting out!**


Do I hear you say you're not ready?  You can't leave <u>yet</u>?
<u>Tha</u>t's a sad song, a song of longing to remain.
    Let's get out!  (You <u>won't</u> stay the same.)
    Come *here* -- rest easy.  Begin the new breaths.

**You ask me: "Who is this unfamiliar person?  (I can't *recognize*
myself.)"**


The person loses her torment?  That is very difficult.  Who is it
that has not got the torment?  (A deep riddle!)
    Go to God.  Search within.  Look at
    the emptiness of the empty place.

**Is <u>that</u> the place?  Empty of what?  What has been lost?  Do you
want it?**


I see you standing at the threshold of a castle you've not yet explored.
Stay and look.  Do you say it's weird?  It's <u>yours</u>!
    <u>Tha</u>t's "emptiness" -- vast cornucopia of unrealized
    riches.  So just *step right up*, Sweetie.

***All*** **yours!  You are *now stepping through the door*.**

## BACK-UP, TURN DOWN, THROWN-OUT BLUES
(Song, after finishing "Black Elk Speaks")


.     .     .


How can I be aware of where we are?
When, momentarily, I know my place
    My spirit shrieks. I've stepped into maelstrom.
    Vertiginous torments seize my kishkes until I back up and

Close the door behind me. That was no place for me!
(Reality sucks.) He or she who looks upon
    the Face of God perishes instantly. *I* would *know* but
    not *suffer* -- unfortunately, that's not how it works.

        **Daylong deadbolt runback daddy**
        **Lost our way, where's the door**
            **(Don't look <u>there</u>, it's dark, there's nothing)**
        **Here's a hallway, roaring to hell.**

           o      o      o


I can't go any further. I'll never be the same.
(You go on without me, and call me when you get there.)
    You have strength, hardiness, hope.
    I'm *here* (halted, hiding).

Looking into the hidden center, I glimpse Hades.
We all do it over and over. The two-legged
    creatures destroy each other. My hopes
    for another way have vanished. I crash.

        **Highbrow songfest hard-knocks Harry**
        **Looked around, then ran for the door.**
            **"Out is out, and I've had plenty."**
        **The roads to "peace" lead to war.**

# TRIPPERS CHOOSE

Celebration (Birthday
of Worlds): I am
Seated
Between
Men of
Substance:


I. *Effector*


Captain of Industry speaks: I can dye
                    your wool green
          So it never fades!  I will make this land *do*
          What *I* want.
          No-one will totally escape <u>my</u>
                    influence!  I
Control these mills --
          They are
          *Mine.*

Yet
I know all my wants and wills
          Resulted from daddy's
                    drilling and smiling insistences,
          From Mom's flickering
                    frowns.
(I, Big Boy, still playing their lines!)

Is it not ironic: All <u>this</u> under
          My "control" -- but what's the key?
          (The code was hidden: who
Holds it? Not I!)

                    Why run the mills?
                    *Whose* mills?
                    All mine -- but I
                    Have no control, as
                    I am run by invisible
                    Laws.

II. *Rejector*


Metaphysician
        presents
        laws
And insists I
        listen and
        obey.

He says my "freedom" to do
        that which I choose is my
        vicious illusion, to be
Stripped away, discarded,
        a frayed veil of no
        further use.

I must face, he says, the
        reality that I
Am merely a machine,
        programmed to
Commit these actions,
        choosing
What I must.

        I ask him why he has
                chosen to tell me this.
        He does not reply.

Then I watch his quiet irritation
        at my choice to talk with
The other man
        at our table (a
Captain of Industry!) who
        seems really interested in my
Questions.

        (Therefore I again
                speak with the controller
        Who controls nothing -- with
                the listener who
        Can't hear.)

III.  *Silent Weaver*


    Later, I tell all this
           to a quiet man, and
    Ask him what it means.

He looks at me, closely,
        watching (apparently)
        how I
Fidget while he says
      nothing.

    He tells me, finally, to
          go away and
    Come back next year
When I have a better question.


IV.  *Evensong*


    But I'm O.K.
    I can't put it together yet
        -- but at least my wife
    Understands it.

    The story, of course,
        is endless. (I forgot the
    Beginning.  This, the middle
        is always
    New and
        strange.)

        How long have we
        Been here?

Isn't it time to
Open the door?


      *     *     *

25

# PATH THROUGH THE MILKY WAY

### I. *Transparencies*

(Let's get on with it!

Is every room just like
Every other?)

Front Door was
long time ago.

Coming through!

(Can we get out?

Is there a
Back Door?)

### II. *Resistances*

When
does the powerplay
Stop?

Who
will go the whole route
Willingly?

(What
time is it in
Mecca?)

Why
have we not yet come to
the End of
Days?

Hallelujah!
The End is near --
I sense compassion
of the world for
each
One.


Please, Lord of Hosts --
Support us. We're

FALLING...

                    *    *    *


          And so
                    There is an end
                         for all --
          And
                    All in all.

     Do we ever come this
                    way a
               Second time?
     I doubt it.



                    III.  *Reprise*

     Captain of Industry,
     Produce the final
               rescue device in
     Quantities sufficient
               for
     Everyone.

     Brilliant Metaphysician,
     Admit you haven't yet thought of
               every answer, and
     Help us to
               find
     A way.

     Wife (dearly beloved),
     Elaborate the music of
               secrets, and show me
     Where I can put my
               foot
     Next.


                    I will choose
                    Choice
                    In each
                    Instant.


                    *    *    *

## IV. *Return?*

Flashwarning:
    "Backup!  Backup!"
    (How do we go back
Up?)

The dream
    is insistent, but
      blocks the view
Ahead.

This dream flaunts
    hereditary Monarchs and
    teaches me that I am not a
Butterfly.

The Ground is
    <u>here</u> -- it's
    hard, and my feet
Hurt.

        Therefore:
        This must be the
        Place.  (Here
           on the
        Ground is
           high
        Enough.)

# 3.

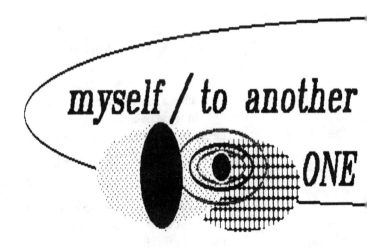

*myself / to another*

**ONE**

**SWING:**

## I. _Exile_ ('58)

I allow and enter my leaving moments
    Always as a Dance.
I am held within--yet hold--myriad brittley movements
    Why am I not (--broken)?


Fragments would glitter and shiver--or would the dust be
    Fine, floating--the shatter
Leaving no trace but a (--dullness
    On) God's or grasses' sheen?


## II. _Return_ ('59)

I remember and end believing movements
    In tense balance.
The dance awaits the partner and will be then transformed
    To scything and gathering.


Will leaning rhythm, the lashing edge allow
    Bent stems to the gleaners?
Or will all grass be left
    Lying for the rake?

## Primal Scene

### I.

I see a lean horse
          mount
A white mare.
Their motion
          burns me.
I look away and run
          (so that I shall not
          be struck to salt).


Once upon a time
I was the vortex
          of creation
And a womb from which
          being sprang
At each instant.

All opened outward
          from my eyes
As I watched
          and sucked
(Vision flowed from
          my eyes over the
          world).


### II.

Now I look
          away
          from the world:
Always---whether watching
          trees
          or faces---gazing
(Gazing down each one's deep
          holes, but
          not seeing to any
Bottom);


Then my gaze becomes
          refuse
Falling (burning---)
          down closed shafts
Towards ash-piles.

And I travel
            always
            through my own
Tiled, self-luminous
            tunnels, that won't end
            in light
Or rain.


### III.

Yet grace comes in glints.

Look!
The shaft walls are cracking---
Drops appear
            at the joints.
(Where are we coming out
Into?)


Watch!
The mountain is opening, and
            the cataracts
            of Spring
Shine.


(But
How can I watch these waters
            without
            growing faint?
For---
When I saw
            the boiling stud
            and the mare---
Sweat rolling off their flanks--- as

They paired, their piercing
Pierced me, and I was wracked
            with uncomprehending
Terror.)

# THE BEING NAMED "TsK"

TsK wishes to feed. The lower realms are full of feeders. Perils of the
waters. The blood-sucker. The voracious shark. Neither wants to harm.
Each needs to feed.
> my blood is food.
> my flesh is food.
I must yield them. I am food.

> TsK demands her feeding. Hungry dreamer. Slow, forgetful hunter.


Perils of woods and fields. Deer-tick waits on the grass-blade, for quarry
to brush by. When will food walk over? Come, submit! TsK waits to suck.
No harm meant -- merely need of nourishment.
> my blood is food.
> my flesh is food.
I must yield them. I am food.

> TsK requests her feeding. Hungry dreamer. Slow, forgetful hunter.


I can serve her purpose as well as anyone, and better than most.
I stand still. I listen. I sympathize. I am aware of her need. I wish her
hunger diminished.
> but blood thins
> flesh pulls back
Why yield them? I will no longer.

> TsK will seek other foods. Hungry dreamer. Slow, forgetful hunter.


Some day again, perhaps, I will submit. I will stand still, listen,
sympathize. Now, I wish some sun, for myself. The corpuscles need
replenishment. The flesh wants rest, easy exercise, strong working. Then:
> blood may again be food
> flesh may again be food
I may yield them again to the feeder.

> TsK thrives, floats, browses. Hungry dreamer. Slow, forgetful
hunter.

# DEAREST BIRTHDAY BOY, THANK YOU!

### for Harmon Ephron (93 years old)

I relish your smile and
voice.  You are the only angelic
old man I have ever known.
(My father also aged with energy and compassion, but
            his flavor was gingery -- fragrant, but <u>sharp</u>.

Your fragrance doesn't bite!)
            Here, I savor a well chewed bite of East European bread.
            The resonances of that taste bind me
            to the old generations I never actually touched -- but yet
they live in me.  Don't stop singing.

            (My father said each person has
            one song.)
            Your song -- melodious, happy-sad -- is
            great gift.  You are
                    *generous* with it!

It isn't simply Klezmer
                (but joy comes through it).
It isn't simply a love ballad
                (though it brims with affection).
It's not merely Lullaby
                (but sooths the child-soul).

            What peace, what a flow of gentle melody.
            The power is there, but doesn't bruise me:
            it is a power that's *resting.*


The ocean waves
            never stop,  their energy
            comes from somewhere deep, from
            everywhere.  Keep on flowing, surging
(listening, reflecting).  Be well!

*34*

## ARCHING TOWARD INFINITY

### for Edith


An anniversary of birth --
four score years (Bonus ten, right?)
All remains the same, yet nothing lasts:

>The bow bent, resisting --
>its fibers generate force
>(pent) to throw  a bolt.

>Yew -- supple, stiff, driving
the fletched shaft     **deep**     **into an intended**
>target.  (The <u>essential</u> deed.)

>Sudden relaxation generates an after-shock.
>The bow, overbent, recovers.
>(The quiver still contains many shafts.)

Spirit, severely stressed
Will not weaken
yet.


## SHE, HAVING LIVED 80 YEARS, IS <u>HERE</u>.

Pure bell rings -
A deafening clamor -
The shining **self** reverberates -
This presence cannot be ignored.
Visual presence also: scintillation; coruscation.
Yet the shine and sound are more than self -- those present vibrate.
Her song and dance tell all of us about happy times, when the great
DINNER
>reigned, a victory for man's and woman's <u>sociality</u>!

>Here the orchestrator is to be **honored**!  Three cheers
>For a mistress of heavenly entertainments -- And let us all
>Wish the seasoned fish server a **happy eighth decade**.

>The great PARTY has begun -- joy in reverberations.
The great social field is shining, scintillating --
All is well with the world, at least until
The final bell, when (unavoidably)
We **all** say "Goodbye".
Until then -
Enjoy!

## PHOENIX, AGAIN

Sam Atkin --
in memoriam


The old coupling ended
            soon.

The new grew
            strong, elastic.

            Discard that painful
                        instrument -- Sing

            rather with this
                        high-energy orchestra.

New music -- forget
            the old.

# Honoring Father, Just Died

### I. Remembering...

He stood fast, steered, dead-reckoned our course.
Took our plunging boat through the surges to safe water.
We tied up, went home, laughed about winds
                    lashing rain, near accidents:
"Almost hit the last buoy!"
                    "Good the motor didn't quit (the way it did
                    the trip before)".

He could hardly see a damned thing, even <u>with</u> his glasses -- but
            he did it anyway.


       \*    \*    \*


He so wanted to get it <u>right</u>, make his mark!  Help the world.
Sometimes he really listened.  Sometimes he talked forever.
            He wanted to figure it all out (a tough job!)
Service did not come easy.  Sustain the effort, he said.
            And he did.  Therefore he served.

        He wowed 'em in Jerusalem.
        Left his mark at Sinai.
His cry traces the wave-crests like a gull.
        The ark of his mind has left the water.
        The animals have debarked:  Each couple
continues its species.  The empty ark rots.

## II. But Continuing...

Arc of mind flings sparks across wave-top after wave-top.
Wind picks up the spray, throws it on the windshield.
        Have to open the window to see what's ahead.
        Gull on the water. (Gull on the water.)

Sorrow. Read the Torah text in yesterday's sunshine
        (I remember it a little). Today, weather
        closed in. (Did you give us the right heading,
Captain?) It's all up to us.

Adrift, today. One of our rudders has broke.
        (Don't tell me I can do it -- I know.
        But it's not the same.)


## III. Wondering...

"Depth". What does that mean? There is water under the water.
And under that mud, holding up the water. And under that rock,
holding up the mud and the water. I can't see any of that, just
the top of the water.
        What sustains the rock?


--1987-

38

# WHAT THE INSCRIPTION DOESN'T SAY

Sam Atkin --
in memoriam


I.

Here's a broad water.
Wind drives the white-caps -- but don't worry!
It's <u>Captain Sam</u> who takes us across.

      * * *   * * *

      Yes, one day...
      Is he
      **gone**
      now, master of crossings?

Laughing!
I remember him best at the wheel,
running an old boat through waves,
squinting to find the elusive buoys (while **I**
gloried in wheeling gulls, in the lift
of water, in the bright shine (clouds, sky).

      * * *   * * *

      One less Captain out there
      now.  But that's how I remember him
      best.

Then there was
**Talking!**
He guided and crafted his sentence
intently -- gave it all he had.
He was <u>there</u> in it, giving his gift.  (<u>Take it</u>! **Sam now**
**centered**
**within this delicate idea** -- the thread of his life.)

      * * *   * * *

      He **wanted**, above all,
      to know the <u>one</u> he spoke with, and **to**
      **be known by that one.**

*39*

II.

Pop -- where are you? *We wrote together!*

       I listened to your words.  You told me, deeply,
about your life.
       It hurt to see you fade.  I admired your strength
to continue --
       your adamant persistence.  Like me, you wanted so much
to **understand**. **How** does the world **work?**

*Who* are **people** -- *this* person?


       Knowing anything is so difficult!  And (toward the end)
you wanted so much to tell me of your discoveries,
       your many small revelations, your very new and
unexpected
**questions,** your glimpses of the mysterious and wonderful...
       You did tell me, for a while.  Then, because of
the inexorable disease process, your voice faded so low
       I could not hear.  Yet
*you kept trying to get across*.

The voice of wisdom -- very, very small...

## ELUSIVE FLYER

### for Shlomo


Bird of Paradise --
    we follow your trail to hidden places
        you teach through your hiddenness


I try to find you --
I watch your crazy flight, trudge to where you have
gone, look around:  What wondrous beauty!  This
flower is opening, and this, and this.


    (Do I fear flowers?
    Is this safety intolerably strange?
    Can I rest peacefully, when you have again
disappeared?)


Then I see you -- flash of feathers, Joseph's coat,
winking flowers up in the green canopy.  I am quiet,
listening:  Your song calls to a bird within me --


        I thank you for my song, a gift from heaven
        My bird within trills, can you hear it?
(Thus Paradise entered me for an instant)

## SHLOMO'S DEEP QUESTION

Shlomo asked
     can the <u>easy</u> route take us to the deep?
Are not "obstacle angels" serving us, guiding our steps
     by blocking them?  I delight in Smoothness, but
Bumps teach better, I'll bet!  It's a delicate question.
     I <u>try</u> not to be seduced by ease.  (But I am,
Anyway.)


The deep questions
     certainly aren't easy!  And the easy answer is that
They're unanswerable.  (Then I can stop bothering my head!)
But
     the <u>question</u> can be stated, can it not?  Is the <u>answer</u>
Another statement?  Or is it a change in the question?
     Or is it, quite possibly, a change in the questioner?  How
Sticky!


(Even when I walk,
     the route with apprehended verticalities brings me more
Satisfaction than smooth, unimpeding concrete.  Whole being
     appreciates the tussle.  I could encounter each
Obstacle with anger.  I could just do the job, thinking about
     something else.  The bottom line, however, is to
Dance!)

# WHO IS BOSS HERE?

"You have done that which I would have you not do.  This comprises
    an attack upon me, which must be
    avenged.  I prepare myself, therefore,
        for battle.
You will see!  You will feel my lance.  It is sharp."


Hardness hurts
    the hurter.  (The shaft slips around the back, and
    catches the warrior
        unawares.
The blow from behind was not
    looked for -- self-inflicted wounds
    weep a plasm devoid of breath.)
Breathing becomes short:  The heart swells
    for battle.  The foe must be found and rendered
    innocuous.


        -=<(|)>=-       -=<(|)>=-


Come -- let us croon the tale of
    anger, unrequited:  The foe won't fight!

  And therefore -- recognition of the warrior becomes
    more and more essential.

    Help for the warrior will come, eventually, in the form of
      narcissistic self-disclosure:

      "You will see shining armor, my sharpened
        lance, and recoil.

        Then (and then only) I will be
        happy!"

# TURN AROUND (LOOK BEHIND)!

### I.
### What
### Hides?


Ricardo mourns incessant
    "never-was", and sounds
Crystal contingencies, crying (oh so
    quietly!) for the lost
Babies, who will not, will never
    be again born, as
His.

He is, therefore, crying
    constantly within, and
Consumes each moment
    avidly, contracting
Frontalis.  Bitter taste, bitter
    effort!  He is
Bitten

By those ancient
    seeds he removes,
Lovingly, one by one from his
    left front pocket to
Chew.  Watch.  With great
    dignity he consumes
Another,

And silently
    cries out: "Another dead
One! Nothing
    will ever
Grow
    for
Me!"

## II.
## Who
## Returns?

Is eating
         this
Dead source
         his real
Nourishment?
         Can Ricardo
Live

Only on this contracted
         food?  What small energy!  Yet
Must suffice!  For if there is
         no other inspiration, then
Regret, lovingly renewed, will
         have to do.  (And remember:
No-one

Ever hears his silent
         cry -- nor does he.  But
Old loss of possibilities,
         consoling him for what he
Did not do, lives in wrinkled
         face, in slow gestures.)
Therefore

Weeping aloud
         has become
Unnecessary:
         Only the deeply
Creased brow remains
         of ancient, crashed
Griefs.

# LESSONS

Child's
eternal cellmate was his tormenting leg.
(This mind, which here
speaks, was raised in that prison. Abscessed bone
      hurts!)
                              Hospital
                        room, white in
                        sunlight, stinks.
                         Games, running beyond
                         normal limits, bounce
                         within raised
                              bedrails.

                              Mind
                        here learns solitary
                        playfulness. Limitations
                        of role recede, except for
                        the doctor-nurse-patient
                        hierarchy, which everywhere
                              dominates.
            Prepare!
Taught to wait, plod, play (to attend unfolding strategies
orchestrated by unseen directors) --
this mind began to plot underground movements, to eventuate in
         escape.
                              Warrior,
                        trained incessantly in
                        the white field, marshalls
                        legions (set to take over the
                        whole stadium), and charges
                        perpetrators of right-leg
                              pain.

                              Battles,
                        freshly sheeted every
                        day, continue. Yet the
                        leg cannot be overcome. Child
                        slowly learns to suffer its
                        stubborn protest, and
                              yielding, wins.
            Osteo-
myelitis set large boundaries; the child,
now grown, is grandiose.
He will entertain the whole world, without
         retreats.

## WRITTEN MOVEMENTS
### (Pressing the Flower)

I.

Poem --
  My guts
Shown
  Before the world.


Now I read this
  Epitaph:
Remember that
  Being?


It rings!
  I vibrate:
The message
  Matches!


(Photo -- of
  My guts spread --
Glistens like the
  Real thing...


That photo
  doesn't
Hum or run --
  But "rings")

47

## II.

Real gut
   also sings,
Arousing
    Reverberations,


And (here!)
   is opening,
To allow
   Flow:


Memorial
   peristalsis
dividing the
   indivisible.


Ah! Watch:
   iridescences
Pulse (worlds pass
   Through.)


Wait: Plunge now
   within the
Whole: read again,
   Glow...

# 4.

*remember*

*our*

*sleepers*

## MOTHER OVER
### (bringing Mother's Body Home)

I.

A very bright child,
   eternally.

Faery tales fed her.
She dreamed, dreamed,
   and dreams.
A beautiful child

So gentle, retiring
   -- and guilty to
   be alive, to be a
   burden on her
   mother ("little girls
   should not be born...")


But she spoke to God,
   and God forgave her.
   So she could live,
   after all.
Up to the very end, this
   cyclical conflict recurred.
She pardoned herself again
   --again and again.  And
went on.

But not today.  Her dance is
   over, on this plane.


II.

She could know something
   and tried with eyes
   large, sharp:
Prey and hunter in one...
   small bird moving
   rapidly, watchful:
And the watching hawk.

It was her way to hide her
   talons, and to ask all
   others to hide theirs...

This vastly reduced the
   threats of war.  The
   Peaceable Kingdom
   seemed almost   around the corner.
The dove cooed its heart out
   And she wept.
She really wanted that peace.
It was the dream of her lifetime.

III.

She knew more than she said.


She was going to tell us when she got home.

It was a bitter-bright story, and would teach a little
Of who she was, and where we were going.
She held it in her mind,
   and left with it.
(Where is her story?)

I say goodbye
To the spirit of the
   story-teller, now
   quiet.  It is a
Long and deep meditation.
   No-mind.  Heart open,

But very quiet.

## FLIGHT WITH COFFIN
### (Bringing Mommy Home)


I will wake you
In my sleep
As we land at
LaGuardia.

Coming down together
Fast, forever, freely.

Please hear my
Whistle of respect
For your glittering lights
And inner visions.

I'm out of the wind
But hear it.
Speech of dumb motion.

You never saw this last glitter
    of the fabulous city
We descend into.
I can't believe the ride.


------------------

Now
We are down.

I'll miss you.

# Simone, Still

in memoriam (10/28-9/88)

### I.

Please flow through the world
leave trails (glistening, sinuous,
    trembling).

Look at this garden:  Partake of harmonies.
Leaves tremble.  Light glitters on
    myriad drops, left from night.

> Sleeping, slipped away
> Softly, left us to
>     mourn.

> Lone, loving: lilted
> tremolos teem, and deep
>     sonorities.

### II.

Deep water.  I see something through the surface.
Beings down there.
    They flicker.

Schooling fish.  Trembling.
Tails flashing silver in unison.
    Darting away.

> You know (knew) such rhythmical
> recurrence, spun melodic
>     gossamer --

> Thus threaded living sounds through
> my being (beads threaded on
>     your song).

III.

I remember (you -- valorous woman, gone but precisely
        here) you -- little girl laughing, stitching our lives.
The luminosity
        of your face inhabits me.  [But how can I tell you?]

            Flow of sounds playing in memory, yet
            gone.  Leaves flash, fall,
                burn.

            Lapping of water; do stars
            reflect from the rippled lake?
            No more.

I know the story by heart.  That you will not be
        back.  My child-mind won't believe, but waits.
You're on a trip.
        Listening for traveller's return (*see*: text reads "never")

I parrot my lesson (*empty*).

# TEACHER'S STRANDS TAUTEN

for Sam Atkin, two years
before his death


Hang in

Hang on

The web stretches:

Each thread has its breaking point


One thread gone -- the web is the same

Another -- a slight shift, but no essential change.

But _that_ one: now the balance is altered (the configuration

is _really_ not quite the same).


The next few seem trivial.

But then: transformation.  _This_ pattern was never here before.

How does it work?  Will it remain?  Wait.

(It's still a web, however.)


Elasticity has its limits...

## FATHER DYING --

Wasted.  Wondrous!  (Withering...)
Limbs have withered.  A quietness.
A crackling.  Something departs, slowly...

(Remember the drying of a leaf:

Was green and resilient --
then browning; the edges curled.
The stem hung, limp.
A brittling began:

Finally, the cutting off at the stem, from
within [scission].)
Now it is almost complete.

He will drop to the ground, melt into it.
We will turn the ground, the new layer under the older.
The crisped body will soften, melt.

But where is he?  Has the man begun to leave?
He leaves, steadily.  No longer green.  He knows he is leaving.
His farewells are silent.  (Hardly a rustle...)  Goodbye!

# DEPARTURE, MYSTERY, WONDERMENT

for Sam Atkin

I watch him carefully.  Now I can see him
easily.  The unchanging is
more visible.  His changing has become so
slow!

I look again:
>     Husk
>     shell
>     shard
>     fragment
>     remnant
>     remainder
> transitory
>         passing
>             shrinkage
>                 (Regeneration?  Return?)

Father
departing slowly
laboriously, with great difficulty.
He was a hard task-master to himself.  Each job continued
with attention to the end.  It must be
done!  On with it...

......... TERMINUS)


Myriad gleaming rails, intersecting in ordered chaos
The train comes in, slows.  The main switch gets cut.

This yard is where routes end, the emptied vehicle gets scoured.
The trip (in past time) contained gleaming vistas, now memory

for riders doing something else now.

I rode that trip too!  How can I forget anything?
The tracks are still there.  (They remind me.)

**TO BE CONTINUED...**


Father in me, I hear you. Your voice is transparent, an echo like dust.
The dust rises in swirls. I remember your beginning, though I was not born.

I remember my beginning, not yet conceived. All has been told to me.
These beginnings in me came as words. They are beginnings in my own world.

Your conjunction with my (now long-ago gone, died) mother,
fathering me, lives in me. I know it, as you knew her.

A deed of creation continued (is continuing,
will continue). I am. Thanks.

## TRANSITIONAL ACTION

Dear Pop
        You held on a long time.
        We held each other, at the end
(hand in hand).

You died simply. I said the Shma and
        You listened intently, then
        Quieted, slowed, relaxed.
You didn't bother to take another breath.

That was it. How easy it seemed to me!
        (The skilled dancer takes his last difficult turn.
        To the untrained observer, such a simple movement!
Behind it, a lifetime of effort, practice. Your skill perfected.)

But why did you stop now? Was this the exact moment?
        You had made, perfected many lives -- loved the dancing.
        (Dancing ends, does it not?) Finis to every perfected compositi
But an encore! (An encore.) I want an encore!

Your life went straight through the most elaborate cycles --
        Circles, spirals of light
        And dark, hunger and satiety.
Was all the sound and fury aimed at the last perfect moment?

Please tell me. I'm left, incomplete --
        An unfinished life. My perfection may await me.
        But I'm so grateful to have been present at your ending
(As you were, in larger role, at my start).

Say whether I will hear and touch you again --
        See your vigorous movements.
        (Actually, I do hear you, because
You are here, though gone.) Say "hello" for me,

        To the nothing or everything you have now.

I thank you for the overlap of our lives.

BABI YAR:
For those murdered long ago

There is a low chasm
    within which many
        lie buried.

"Lead me to those graves"
    I asked the clean youth with pens.
        He did, sweetly, then

left.
    There was a picnic table.
    We prayed.

# WHAT HAPPENED?

in memoriam
(Minnie Finkelstein
1905-1987)


Oi Minnela! Trickster of the world. Great Magician!
You have pulled the disappearing act of the Century.
    Last week, your presence spoke volumes --
    Your steely vibrations impaled us everywhere,
Passed through us, impaled our kishkes ( -- a suffering

Daughter testified, with long, bitter love.) Minnela
Everywhere. The intensity, however, crescendoed
    As the wary visitor approached 30-46 73rd Street.
    That unique locality was the center of Minnela-World.
There we worshipped love-hate intensities, your stream of

Words. One day, last week, you introduced us,
    your admirers, to your plan: Changing planes
    by a complex, unannounced sequence of transformations.
It was miraculous! First you began a deep and resonant

Simplification. You congealed your vast array of words into
    A cry. (Did you remember the cry of Arrival? Was this
    The cry of Departure?) Then search, thirstiness,
The restless touching everywhere. Rapid breathing:

Then the peak, running, running (no breath). And so, you
    Succeeded in changing our whole world...
    Ultimate trickster -- Minnela! has entered all
Our drawers, locked and unlocked -- stolen those vibrant echoes

We had secreted therein. What brashness! You, now, the
    Thief in the night! And: disappearance of all those
    Steely vibrations. What remains? A peace (that
Passeth Understanding). Your repose permits limber sadness

In our slowed hearts, the shaft of sharp words removed forever.

# SAFARI

And now here we are, folks, in a New World! It's the After-the-Passage
existence of <u>Survivors</u>. What a burden! What a <u>blessing</u>. Landing was a
<u>blast</u>! And now Onward into an unknown continent, toward pacific
shores, another ocean. What lies ahead? Mystery after mystery (and no
more
mother as guide, commentator, complainant, or kvetch-specialist).

\* \* \*

(God drives a hard bargain. The contract requires that we talk to
each other, study our route, plan a suitable itinerary, and begin.
It will be possible to compensate for losses along the way, with
God's help.)

Let's get our expeditionary forces together: We need plenty of <u>supplies</u>.
The length of the Journey is totally unknown, and the trip will be, it is
absolutely sure, unlike any of our dreams, no matter how outrageous.
Therefore it is essential to <u>see</u> ("Look where you're going! Watch your
step"). How unlike the previous landscape! Prepare.

(Actually, the places are not so different, but the travelers are.
The child ran through a forest of vast adults. It was amazing! But
it all shrank down to a cruddy playland, with no more giants. Then
<u>parents</u> transmigrated -- stepped out of this plane, with no
apologies. And <u>now look</u> where we are! I never saw the landscape
here with this light on it. Am I crazy? Or was all this here
all the time, but I wouldn't look? ...Take me away while I'm still
conscious.)

\* \* \*

Nightfall. All landscapes look the same without light. Sleep is
delicious. The soul needs refreshment. Retreat is necessary. Then we
can go on.

# COMING TOGETHER

## Separation:

There was the wall. The stones had been piled and grouted.
The lines of grout had hardened -- had they not?

And no-one crossed over. There was no door. We found chinks
To call through. It was hard. We could not see each other.

## Stagnation:

Cold weather came. Winter froze the remaining buds and branches.
Nothing was growing any more -- the ground white, beautiful, bare.

Calls had ceased. Then, the long wait.
Silence...

-- II --

## Reparation:

But came the Magician! Minnie Quick-Changer:
"I will become **Separation**! I will become **Stagnation**!

I will disappear! (taking separation, stagnation with me). You
Can come Together to look for me. I am gone. (Remember.)"

**The very next day, we found the door.** The spring sky, beautiful blue.
Tree buds began to open. (Where did you go, Minnie?)

# MOTHERLESS

The Mother:
    Heavy, dark, sharp,
        twisting (a spewer
        of venom);

The daughter:
    Sleek, bright, hard,
        trim, true (hunting
        jewels).

Suddenly, mother lifts,
    Shifts her weight --
        climbs out of our space here
        Forever.

The daughter, who was
    tormented by the cutting
        explosive
        presence --

Is now tormented by the sudden
    inexplicable inexhaustible
        and totally unprecedented
        absence.

# ANOTHER MESSAGE FOR THE ONE WE REMEMBER

You were strong
        sturdy
        and never silent--

There has been no other like you in my long experience,
        and I would not trade the privilege of having been around
        while you slowly exploded for all the tea in China.

You were the envoy, to
        Jackson Heights, from
        the world of my forefathers.

The language you spoke was full of mysteries,
        fragrant, troubling, turbulent. Yet
        totally plain. You knew that everyone knew what you knew.

So how is it possible to continue here, without your voice?
        Your story does not leave. (This Spring, without Minnie
        watching children through her window, is therefore less green.)

I stay here for a few minutes, now, recalling
        the many years you remained upright
        and held your place strictly, speaking truths.

I hear you, Minnie -- lacking guile! You (childlike)
        don't know that words you say are not exactly
        those I hear. (How can you not suspect a difference?)

You will remain, for me, an enigma of crystal clarity.
        I recall your hallway. I watch you descend your staircase,
        with measured determination, to unlock the door.

## WE LIVE HERE, NOW -- DO WE NOT?
### (Ceremony in a graveyard)

Her story over
Yet here we are
This too is her story

    This place -- so quiet!
       (Drums and butter, no more.)

The story seemed endless.
    It grew light, and dark.
    Lightning and Thunder.
    Snow and sun.

       World whirling toward everywhere, with
          nothing to show for it.
       Or is there something, after all?
       (Is it just a long intermission?)

    -=|=-   -=|=-     -=|=-   -=|=-

    Let's get on with remembering!
    How can we not remember?
    Yesterday just happened -- is it already lost?
What will become of us all?
Why are we here?

(The sad fact is that nothing matters
    unless we recall our reasons for
    being here. So let us be here, all together, in harmony, strongly
standing upon the ground of our unknown destinies. These will not be lost.)

Don't go -- I love you. Watch
    that flock of birds, twisting, swirling above the tombstones.

      **This moment, as we are now, is her lega**

## UNVEILING THE STONE OF REMEMBRANCE

This is a day for remembrance.
   The new tiny one in the Pale, remembered
      The girl hungering for apples --
         The Greener struggling to earn bread.


The woman now, holding her own two girls, watching everything carefully.
No Cossacks here!  **This** was
         a <u>safe</u> place -- (except...  And except...  And except...)

This stone was cut to show
   when she came
      and when she left.
         Look!  Last year she made her grand exit.


A twin stone now, recording two souls who travelled light, for a long time.
These two went everywhere together!  **One** house
         their <u>only</u> place -- (except...  And except...  And except...)

We are a gathering of survivors.
   We came to let each other know we remember
      the new tiny one, the girl hungering, the Greener --
         The woman passing through, bearing fruit, saying Goodbye.

Stone
To remind us
         to remember.

# 5.

DOWNBEAT

# RHYTHM

Dance the tune
    The piper calls
Who doesn't dance
    To limbo falls.

Who doesn't dance is
    Danced and spun
Till feet fly up
    And dancing's done.

----------

Dance your day;
    Call your tune.
(Ring around the rosey-O!)

Sing your lay;
    Silence soon.
(Who will have my poesy-O?)

## SURVIVING --
### (Swimmer, way out)


Awake?
      How tired I've grown.
      My tissues cover
bone.

(Will ocean
      buoy brain?)
      To swim needs
pain

Goading
      me to reach
      Land (a rain soaked
beach).

Hurts
      too sharp for soothing
      can penetrate
dozing

I labor
      to land
      (to touch
sand)

## PARTY: HUDSON RIVER

Ride the great fun boat.
(Hear the ponderous choo-choo!)

       The river calms and quickens:
            -- sharp foldings race and ride
            -- slow waves flash blades at our heels.

       A ripple wind (Spring's hide, fleshed),
       Stitched with the shore's chatter,

       Rejoices.


Voices:

       A rhyme skin stretched over clash of couplings
            (and uncouplings)
            (and rattle of trucks in a hidden yard)
       Becomes the bridegroom's clamorous May.

Now a joyous dancing!        --tumbled by the rolling deck
Now a high-wind singing!     --sibilant, pierced with cries
            (the unrepentant damned? the gulls?)
       From grinding train tires
       Riding (God-forsaken)
           the willful, gleaming rails.

## GOING AWAY

Ducks in gloom
    roam the shore
    (I leave a room
        and close my door).

    *

They dive for seeds,
    and don't complain
    (then down the stairs,
        and into the rain;

    *

The rain will enter
    the rooms I've left):
    A duck's a sifter
        (I'm bereft).

# WATCH THE HUNTER

(about L)


She
   (the harpy --
   razor-taloned)
dives at the cool fish:
   slashes,
   wounds (my flesh).

The cut hurts sharp (but heals --
   the tear seals, then disappears).


I glide,
   (wait),
      expect,
         experience,
            (regret), forget
               each attack. After each,
the bird in the sea
   glistens, glows (its anger burned), preens,
     (drinks), rises,
       flies again, circles.
       (Gull's grace, and <u>serenity</u>.)


I watch, marvel, admire,
   do my work,
   and wait. (The hunger will be on her soon,
   she will hunt:
she will spot my slow, easy glide,
   anger will flare
      viciously: thus, another tearing dive.)

     But now, **two beings are beautiful and apart.**

     The moment sings.

Slippery
Sliding
Singing
Resilient                Sibilant
Brilliant                          Sorry
Ebullient              Sad
Saxophoner
Socratic
Sedulous

Sarcophagus
Sword
Sordid

**Swell**

**Swat**

**Sweet**

**Slurred**

**Singing**

# INNOCENT QUESTIONS

===============

How does one keep the

    Ends together?  How will
        this in-dwelling world
    Disengage from the vasty
        patternings of eternity?

(I'm afraid I'll forget the whole thing.)

Can I see, sense any
    eternal verities?  Look at
    scenes (remember others):

Here we have it!  *These* may be eternal.

===============
### Formations
    Rock --
    Word --
    (Glider?)
    (Bomber?)

===============
### Conflagrations
    Drygrass
    Woodstove
    Endlife

## SEVEN ESSENCES


*ALL*

    *PARADOX*


       *WAITS*

             (*within*)

*THIS*

    *LONELY*


     *NOTE*

### I Don't Age But

The world around
Grows younger, as
Friends die.

### I'm Not Leaving -- Although

The scene changes
(It all moves into
Eternal Goodbye).

### The Consequences of This Moment

Remain beyond my
Grasp, which grows more
Gentle.

### I Stroke All Sights, Finding

Nuances, infinitely
Soft, receptors that
Return my touch.

### I'm Not Leaving -- Although

The scene changes
(It all moves into
Eternal Goodbye).

### I Don't Age But

The world around
Grows younger, as
Friends die.

# OLD ONE

The old one
      hangs on. Is
      age history?
Or proof of worthiness?

      "I count my age
           (forever)
          from
My beginning.

      That which lasts
         has value.  This old
         one merited
Preservation."

What fantasy!  Being
      still here is
      purely accidental.
Many, far worthier, left early.

So what does age
      prove?  Only that
      this year matters.  Its
Fruit falls, tastes sweet.

Each bite precious, savored, the
      finitude of chewing
      becomes
The new Revelation.

(Words chewed
      endlessly become
      a last year's
Legacy.

Age is counted ahead, from
      beginnings.  What
      is counted back, from
The end?)

# HEAVY PIANO MOVING

How can I not marvel at
Ponderosity!  My bones are shaken.
This is not a fantasy.  What does the
        Concept of "piano" have to do with this
            Obdurate mass?

Here is Pearl's Piano
Refusing (with Gravitational assistance) to
    Move in.

Two young bull-men, hearts
        Pounding, shove
        Against this black
Majesty, all intent to raise her.

Muscle fails: Hill does not permit!  Precariously
Balanced, Piano
        Teeters on our hillside
Slide, yet will not be slid up.  The utmost

    Strength of
Two does not suffice.  And
When Pearl and I join and push, Piano budges
    Slightly:  But the slope is
        Too steep.

See: No sly strategy suffices to
        Attain the
        Goal.  Do we
Telephone, confer, give in?

        Yes.  This
Struggle touches my heart.  Weight
    Wins.

It will not go!
    Reload the
    Truck, take
The piano back.

---

(What a heaviness!  In New York, the piano, abused, will be
    checked and repaired.  Next week a larger crew will bring it
    a second time.  We trust they will get it into the house, and
    install the piano in its prepared space.)

# INVISIBILITIES

Postulate
Two REALMS
Within a world.
      Each may be very large
      (one, no doubt,
      larger than the other).
They are different continents, separated by ocean.
There is no radio. Nothing human flies.
Ships do not cross the vast water.

Dwellers of one realm
      suspect nothing of the other.
      (This _my_ continent, disbelieved by _them_!)
---- **Can I imagine such deep ignorance?** Not easily.

Their ancient fantasy my reality. (These
      hard stones were
      hidden from them, therefore
Unreal.)


Postulate
Two LANGUAGES
Within one realm,
      each expressive
      (though deeper tides tug
      from one than from the other).
Two systems of thought, everywhere incommensurate.
No speaker of one language knows the other.
Each hears the other's speech as racket.

Speakers of one tongue
      cannot conceive intelligence
      in those who speak the other.
---- **Can I imagine such deep ignorance?** Not easily.

Their disinterest is my reality. (My
      piercing talk was
      hidden from them, therefore
Unreal.)

Postulate
Two NATIONS
With one language.
        Each may be busy
        (though one
        quieter than the other).
Cohesive crowds split, disjoin this single world.
Cry out for easy banter -- every word glints fear.
Warships cross our vast water.

I inhabit one realm,
        know nothing of the other
        (though dreaming of threats and uniforms).
---- **Can I imagine such deep ignorance?**  Not easily.

Mystification, projected, simulates
        reality.  (All remain
        hidden away, therefore
Unreal.)


Postulate
Two GENERATIONS
In the same nation,
        each exquisitely expressive, disdainful
        (young intensities
        exceeding old).
Two systems of thought, everywhere disparate.
Each speaking, hardly hears the other.
Is duration all?  (Can word cross water?)

Each age molded within one realm
        speaks ill of the other,
        wills not to wonder, hides contempt (as: bored).
---- **Can I imagine such deep ignorance?**  Not easily.

Is your dream my reality?  (Are
        my reviled treasures
        hidden from you, therefore
Unreal?)

Postulate
Two BEINGS
In the same generation.
     each may be very expressive
     (though one
     more than the other).
Two systems of thought, everywhere hiding.
Each speaks, but hardly hears the other.
A word drifts, crosses vast water.

The dweller of one realm
     will not know the other
     (yet dreams, imagining the foreign shore).
---- **Can I imagine such deep ignorance?** Not easily.

Is your dream my reality? (Are
     my hard hungers
     hidden from you, therefore
Unreal?)


Postulate
Two EXPLORATIONS
Within one being,
     each busy within me
     (though one
     quieter than the other).
Pathways, contiguous but split, never meet.
There is no rebuke. No voice between realms
Speaks. (Speech will not span these waters.)

I wake and dream within one continent,
     know nothing of the other
     (though remembering a distant land).
---- **Can I imagine such deep ignorance?** Not easily.

Phantoms orchestrate this search. (Explorer
     hides the routes; clues
     caught in frayed threads remain
Unreal.)

Postulate
Two MEANINGS
Guiding one exploration,
      each expressive of ultimate ends
      (though one may be
      deeper than the other).
Two systems of thought, reciprocally transcendent.
No expression of one meaning repels, ejects the other.
Each bears the other's spirit as precious.

I respond to one tongue
      as the essence of intelligence
      yet try also to hear the other.
---- **Can I accede to my deep ignorance?** Not easily.

Unfolded meanings are my reality. (My
      hard stones stand
      within both worlds, unyielding, and
Real.)

# 6.

## Special Occasions

# SEA-TREE ANNIVERSARY

Pearl's & Adam's 5th


(Garden)
Five years packed
with Done and Undone.
See each other's essences?  When?
Sometimes I reveal roots
and branches to your loving touch.
-- Prune, then, the deadwood without
harming the quick.


(Ocean)
Lets go!  Sweetie Pie --
And dive into surf.
New waves roll in
from the horizon.
-- Everything is on its way
Here.


(Future)
Five more years to bring
strange stories:  Witches, hobgoblins,
Archangels and heavendelights
at every turn.  When we don't
-- Doze, every moment will
Astonish.


(Ocean)
This wave we are in rolls us over
into our next moment.
It faces me at heaven, then pulls
me to sea-floor shells.
-- You and I surface
together, and swim!


(Garden)
A pair of trees, we twine, each trunk
resilient.
-- The wind bends us, and we
dance.

(for Pearl)

*H*ow
    *A*re we to
        *P*ractice
            *P*eace,
                *Y*et not

    *B*urden each other
        *I*n
            *R*eaching
            *T*oward
                *H*eaven?
              *D*on't
                  *A*sk!   (It's not eas
                *Y*)

# CONGRATULATIONS, SISTER!

for June (on her birthday)


June's finger traces greenery-
lace and tendrils of veins.
She feels the laborious innerwork
of forming bodies.  These generate themselves
with insistence.  Sweet solitude, working
to flow a universal calligraphy
into heart's harbor.


Hello, June!:
Please draw a line for me!
I await your birthday,
present to the subtle link
of the one mother who wouldn't wait.
Tracery, wreathes, a headstone --
all fix the date, yet race along ...


I see you stopping soon,
turning toward yourself.
Becoming the June who births
dayfigures of plantlifes and childbreaths
on white rectangles, every day.
Daybirth marches on!  Junie
don't cry ...

## MINDS MARRIED? -- I DON'T MIND!

for Pearl's & Adam's 6th anniversary

### I.

This is it
Again -
Can we love each other
    recognizing that which
    will not be recognized
    with ordinary eyes?

I wish to become quiet
While touching my
Self
    and you will be
    the air of my immersion,
    the silence of birds singing in leaves.

    Please stay:
    I wish to stay.
But stability is pain.

    If I stay
    I change
(But by running remain

    The Robot Adam).
    That which grows
Remains planted.

If only the contact between us could last
    for more than an instant!
If only we were able, simultaneously, to
    bear the pain of waiting!

### II.

    My heart swells as we work
    Separately, and I
Listen to your movements.

    Sun through the leaves
    At our windows
Generates longing and loneliness.

    Dear God!  Life is good.  Yet
    I hardly know
My place.  This planet plunges

Toward war.

### III.

Dear God. Grant me this day
A moment of understanding.
I can hardly wait any longer.

I come crashing down. How often
Do I listen to you?
To listen I must be silent.

And wait.

### IV.

Pearl becomes the wildness and silence
of the world
An atmosphere without clear boundary (an ocean
of despair and elation:

I am the swimmer
I feel the water
I am upheld
I breath the air
and burn.)

The sky is everywhere:
Out and up --
Blue, luminous, omniscient.

My refuge is
our life
as we fight,
breathe,
sleep,
and float

here.

## ROUND

for Pearl (on her
50th birthday)


I

Roundelay to a round day.
All my life with you flows
into the same source
and all begins again.

Eternal endlessness.
Each moment births itself
indescribably, in the blink
of an eye!  I wish to toast

Eternal adolescence!  We will
grow into a new phase relentlessly.
It hurts!  How confusing!  Yet
not to begin again is to

Slide (unastounded) into sunlit sea.
Sorrow comes from the sun's compassion
for vegetable life, out of which
mean animal possibilities arise.

## II

I regret:  That we don't
interpenetrate with exquisite
tenderness (hand in water;
tongue in mouth) more often.

Yet:  All that is allowed to us
by our convoluted structures,
we experience.  I cry with helplessness
at my inability to remember.  What?

That we have that which is needed
but forget that we have it
or forget what it is for.
Please remember with me, when you can!

## III

Be still.  Slide this way.
Lie quiet against me.  Hear o Israel!
We can become
One prayer in praise of flesh.

Marriage is art in situ.
Consecrate this gentle heat
now burning off dried angers,
to the process that seeds our original existence.

I love our confluence.
Grass sings outside the window.
Years flow forever.  Our century,
half over, brings continual surprise.

## VALENTINE SUNSHINE

for Pearl

:::::::::::::::::::::::::::::::::::::::::::::::::::::::::::::

I'll tell you a story
about a little boy
who walked far along a road
admiring all the filigree/diatomaceous traceries
of verdure everywhere, even underfoot

Until a bus came, he got on, and lost contact with that stuff
almost forever.

:::::::::::::::::::::::::::::::::::::::::::::::::::::::::::::

Our lives change.
We pull in, push out, turn and turn again.
That's the answer!  Just stay with it.  Here it comes again!

:::::::::::::::::::::::::::::::::::::::::::::::::::::::::::::

I give you my promise that I will be
someone with
whom
it
will
be possible
to congregate on Sundays to watch a parade
of Hindu elephants graze down Fifth Avenue, speaking slow moons
and saxophones.  It has been done before.
WE will do it again.

In the meantime --
HAPPY ST. VALENTINE'S DAY!

--- With much love
and joy
and sadness

(this is my stop)

## BIRTHDAY WISHES

for Pearl

Touch frees my lust to lubricate and excite
    love, so inner that I become
    hard, shining, healed.
All talks to me within.  I want your
    sweet lips to soften, mine to receive
    the nectar of each day's, each moment's
Arising.  I am born anew as I taste
    your being, and know my place
    with you.  Our births opened into
Two flowing worlds, now confluent.
    Can we know our own beginnings?
    That knowledge will crown each end.
I bear and am born now, hear your
    heart and voice, wish to hold you
Forever.  Be calm, smooth, happy, whole.
    On your birthday.  Always.

## BIRTHDAY GREETINGS

for Pearl


Sweetheart, your breath and vigor thread through my existence.

Life loves us. Birthdays are beautiful symbols of life's core.

Growth and birth, indescribable! Consummate artistry in each jot.

The whole, a miracle. And the transition from this instant's

Miracle to the next instant's miracle: Infinite mystery.


So stay and be born here again

Every instant

Telling me

Sometimes

How you feel

Now

and now

and now.

# FOR MY PRECIOUS PEARL

(on Valentine's day eve)


Inner music trembles and chimes. We have
  so much to give each other
and do. Come back! Stick around!
  Vibrate! Let's harmonize.
That long breath flows almost forever.
  And the pulse. Beautiful.

*Here (one) here (two) here (one) here (two)*

So now we have our symphony
  in operation. You play a sweet tune,
to my drums. The bouncing is
  delicious (nothing harsh now).
Improvise. We drift with ecstatic
  abandon.

*I thank you for my pleasure.*

And for yours! You've a doozy of a
  glide. Sweet strolling among
the leafless trees. Their buds swell
  silently. Muted crooning, thin slides,
and syncopated laughing. I love this
  piece! Thanks (and please

*Don't stop).*

# ANNIVERSARY

for Pearl and Adam


**Ten years** -- This time continues, ceaseless.
　　　This marker in the flow is
　　　just for fun, the
　　　tinsel balloon that
　　　rises into the clouds.  Glitter
　　　here, then gone.


**Tender** -- Swooping silences, hiding significance
　　　(seeds).  Harbors in rain.  Luminous ocean
　　　wonders, spray glittering.  The deep fish
　　　moving from sun to shadow.  It all glows
　　　(grows) -- takes the invisible ray and
　　　gives back indescribable shimmer.


**Tension** -- Hear the paradoxes!  I will not give what I haven't
　　　got.  I cannot see that which refuses to hide,
　　　but rage to capture the beast that won't leave
　　　it's lair within me.  Therefore: truth is torn,
　　　ragtag citizens of cold nations dance without
　　　partners.


**Tree (and flowers and field)** -- Settling here, surrounded by leaves.
　　　Green brilliance, dancing.  We dwell in splendour,
　　　awaiting another second.  Tensions (sometimes)
　　　reconciled, tenderness (sometimes)
　　　recreated, we bask in gifts: Feel the radiance!
　　　Hear the birds!  Say "hello"!

# HAPPY 54 AND MANY MORE

for Pearl (on her birthday)


Sweetie -- you are a Trouper!  The crazy
                    surprises come
And here we are.  (Not exactly what we
                    planned, is it?)

        Thanks for hanging around -- for
                    hanging out with me!
        What we see is what we get.  (And what we
                    don't see, we get also.)

Getting it together, however, is a whole
                    different ballgame.
(Of course, ballgames are not my cup of tea.)
                    A swing is not a hit.

        So the adventure develops -- one damned
                    surprise after another.
        It's a Marx Brothers howler!
                    A Charlie Chaplin tear-jerker!

And you're my Leading Lady -- so it's all O.K.
                    (A gas.  A ball!)
One more year on the boards completed.  The next
                    will be uphill all the way...

        But fun -- the game's fantastic!  We plunge along,
                    trying to stay awake
        and to see what's up.  (You serve as eyes in the
                    back of my head, and

Vice Versa.  It's all complementary.)  Let me never forget
                    to complement you.
Gratitude is love's favorite costume.  Thank you for being
                    here, where


        I am.
                Your essence enters, continues, flows.
                I thank you again.
                    And wish you a glorious 54th!

## SLIDING THROUGH SURF, CAST UP ON THE BEACH.

**for Pearl (our 11th anniversary)**

### I.

Anniversary Shag! We're heading in, digging through.
Now <u>out</u>. There's the light... Charge ahead: sprint leap --
    then twist to get feet under
    for the landing. Let's <u>do</u> it! (do it... do it... )

The landing <u>worked</u>. We hit the dock together and
stand <u>here</u>, amazed. I follow you through
    now. Walk ahead (skip!
    I grab you... we whirl...)

The new story is totally unknown to me. We head
across a wide water under a power we have not tested
    before. Your visage radiant, you show me another
    life. Step aboard -- crank up -- shake loose

And run. This too is a high heading. Gulls cry.
We're moving along. We're nearly there
    (slide through the deep water... slip
    along above the mud...)

### II.

Tie up. Step out. The dock still stands.
Rough boards. The place is rugged.
    Is the place different but the direction unchanged?
    Or do we go differently, though in the same place?

I've seen this before, but very slow.
The instant change is astonishing! Do you see that flash?
    The fish jumped. Now it's all gone.
    Let's go home.

## III.

Boat cuts, surges, rises.  Motion drawn
far down, pressed far up.
Sea supports our lives.  We draw together and
apart, a surging motion.
      Earth moves around the sun.
      We twist.
      We hold each other afloat, floating,
      a silken swim.

The last moon slims down to nothing.
I watch you entranced, see
your inner tides --
we ebb, we flow.
      Have we slid into the channel?
      The new moon grows.
      What magnificent scenery.
      (Waves slap and suck.)

And we -- still holding together.  What a
miracle!  Move with me still.
Slide into the waves, roll against me.
I love your audacious harmonies --
      I treasure your swift trills
      and triplets.  Water melodies.
      We continue singing together.
      I try to find the chord.

**God loves.**

# 62 SUMMERS AFTER BEING BORN


Sixty-two!  A new view.
    None of this stuff ever happened to me before.
    I'm still waiting for Messiah.  But look around!
This must be the place!

However, I do have trouble seeing it.
    Going to the ophthalmologist didn't help much.
    The nuisance floater drifts and jostles.
As the mote moves I see my place, interrupted.

Hello!  Who's there?  (Hearing's not so hot either.)
    The view, nevertheless, crystallizes, and
    The noise orchestrates.  What this place
Loses in turbulence, tumult, it gains in mystery.

The sea.  (Here I am.)  Wherever I go, the sea.
    This shore, where I stand, supports me.
    I look out -- How deep?  I look down.
What illusions!  The bottom recedes miraculously.

I look into this present landscape.  Where is its horizon?
    I see it.  But it recedes.  All pushing back, as I watch.
    The more I look into it, the further away the end gets.
Patience yields fortitude.  I await the receding terminus.

Said Don Juan, "remember that death sits on your shoulder".
    This monkey here interrupts my drowsing!
    The ear-nip is a great nuisance -- but then,
Why not!  I'll stay at my party, and sleep later.

What makes it all worthwhile is the element of surprise:
    God has engineered the world so that
    No two moments coincide in any way!  Therefore:
This right now can't congeal, because it has already disappeared.

            * * *  * * *


("My life" as idea is abstraction.  My life as story is miraculous!
    My partner, Pearl, enters into my substance.
    Our story fascinates and entertains --
The scenery is shifting, the next act, not yet rehearsed, starts.)

# SOUP OF THE EVENING, BEAUTIFUL SOUP!

Harmon Ephron, 94 years old


-- == << (( ||| )) >> == --


I savour sparkling broth, rich in
flavor, quiet upon the table, resting
calm, rich beyond measure.

> Does time become thinner, more clear?
> (the consomme strained, tinting light
> without scattering it?)


-- == << (( ||| )) >> == --


Your being (patiently delighted) allows
each drunken existence to exist
according to its own lights.

> That is a genius of acknowledgement: to entertain
> knowledge of separate being, all the while
> being entertained by illusions of separation.


-- == << (( ||| )) >> == --


What clarity of sight!  In your presence
I am seen, and each present particle
glories in reflecting light.  Watch!

> Continuation of presence blesses your friends,
> as you support them by seeing.  I bless your
> presence -- may it long continue!

## TWO-FOLD LIFE

for Pearl on
our anniversary


The time has not
      run out. The held
Note has neither
      beginning nor
End. I am thankful.

This tiny world, so much
      of which you've made,
Is perfect: I am held here
      by your gifts, your
Generative spirit.

            This captivity is
                  lovely, giving
            Great nourishment;
                  don't forget
            To return continually.


      *        *        *


            I wish to rest here,
                  renewed with your
            Breath, breathing deeply
                  of airs that support
            My candle's burning.

Your burning illuminates
      this page. And
Singing can be read
      from it; a flaming
Duet: Sing! I burn too.

            The time has not
                  run out. The held
            Note has neither
                  beginning nor
            End. I am thankful.


*103*

## BALLAD MARKING 12 YEARS
## (THE SIMPLICITY OF REMAINING)

for Pearl on
our anniversary


**This is a greatness easily**
**forgotten:  To bring ice**
**crystals together,**
**Melt them!**

And so: It is exactly our
Inconstancy
that has sustained
Our commitment.

What a simple paradox:
To attain continuity,
how much can I change?
I will change constantly!

(As we are each
always new --
So will our connection
endure.

**Changing**
**Each instant: Cohering**
**Fluidities.  All touching is**
**Instant surprise,**
**Continually.)**

\*     \*     \*

We have discovered this Law of Love:
Do not stay constant; do not
freeze memory and image; just
Listen!  Just look!  Just
Touch!

I salute you!  Hello my
great friend.  Please
Continue to surprise me, as
you have done constantly from
Day One.

**This largeness**
**of our intention**
**never ceases**
**To amaze me.**

**You and I (echoing)**

for Pearl


Here!
remember
stay again.

Two yet one
separate yet undivided
linkages ephemeral yet eternal.

Connections that shift every instant yet never change
bindings that propel each to move differently, further than ever dreamed
constraints that allow miraculous slippage.

The coming together has held
each being holds the other
so two stay quietly.

Quietness shouts
holding speaks
Hear!

## FOR A WEDDING

Youngsook and Ken

### I. FEAST

This joining brings joy.  Each
    grows from
    the other's
ground.  Is spirit separable?

Were those who are joining ever
    apart?  Or
    were they
touching before (but more gently).

Look at their luminescence!  Clearly
    they have long
    been preparing
this shining EVENT!

And how long can touch continue?  Sense
    the everlasting
    shaking (their pulse-
beats), felt within.

So! Stroke of bow on string
    evokes
    sustaining
vibration.

Song breeds beings -- lives
    hidden,
    coming to
light.

## II. FOREVER...


Unseen beings reveal
Themselves, presences
Unborn, yet breathing
Infinitely delicate air.

Two are linked to bear
Separation: Future
Lives cannot be brought
Before their time.

Loss: waiting
Means loss. Waiting
Is loss continually, yet
Always the new comes.

Wait for losses, yet all
Will be here. Joy
Contains losses.
All leaves forever,

Yet
Is
Always
Here.

## III. CHERISHING

Flashes of fun:

Something new
is always ready!

Can the loved being
ever
be known?
No!
But the looking
But the listening
Is the power to remain
with
ungrasped being.

* * *

Prepare for the shift
Prepare the surprise
The unacknowledged vibration is the important one
It is the matrix for what is seen and heard.

Look more closely
Watch the shimmer hidden by the wave
Be patient -- attend to rustlings
(does an ant walk inside this flower?)

Remember
that the longed-for image
will be very subtle.
Remember
that the longed-for noise
will be faint.

That which two, coupled
but unbound, want to
tell each other, with
eye and mouth, is
less easy to know, but
will be known.

## STEADY STAR (TWO FATES TOGETHER)
for Pearl on St. Valentine's Day


------------------
*A long time coming,*
*flying high.*
*A long time going*
*(shining sky!)*
------------------

Hey--wait a minute:


Where is the still point between bodies
about which we turn?
Binary lights
mutually orbiting --
(What gazer detects our periodic occlusions?)


Paired movement marvelously regular, yet
always in a new place:
Close encounter
means hard tugging --
(What angel guides these revolutions?)


Our coupled history has rhythm, ongoing
but never the same:
Unique movement
marvelous in constancy --
(Shall continual change generate silence?)


Trace one trajectory, double line, racing
through constellations.
Perspectives, from
eyes-in-flight, transform
(Can each see the other, and not grow faint?)


OK--finish the song:


--------------------
*The stars remember,*
*we're here, our turn.*
*It's cold December*
*(love's fires burn!)*
--------------------


*109*

**7.**

*making / maker*

# guidelines

Watcher's poem
**Carved**
     catches drifting lights of hours,
       of seasons:
    folds out skilled fingers, and
        ---as distant hill
        ---or sky
Moves with each viewer, coming along.


Wanderer's poem
**Painted**
    winds the sun-bright, wheeling world
      with shadows:
    in soaring fullness
       ---of far hill
       ---or sky
That follows, follows when one has gone.


Winnower's poem
**Chanted**
    rushes motion into motion;
      word timbres rumble:
    gathering earth and wind song
      ---for hill dance
      ---a cry
To toss then blow the drying tongue.


Wonderer's poem
**Found lone**
    is lightened bone, spiralled shell
      dune gathered:
    thrown, flung hard
      ---to hill
      ---to sky
To sail / sound / bound / and roll.

# EBB AND FLOOD

Tree
  moves its sap and tendrils
  with a fineness like the drift of sands;

Flows
  are tight-pulled strands
  that lace its life.

Tender tip
  of creation, green fountain--
  it mounts the universe it makes:

Then slowly leaps,
  spraying bright cascades
  of buds
          and of buds
                of buds.

## BUILDING

The live tissue
              is frail
And falls away.

Gratitude, love are moments
              grown
              and historied
Which the grave
Takes easily and well;

While hate endures
              strong
              as stones---

Monuments are made of it.

The intellect a granite tower?
              ---or an apple tree?

Mine, a scaffolding of brittle sticks
              and green sticks, lashed
              with vines and twine.

Climbing it gives a local view
              of
              a waterfall (the  scattered water flashing
              among late sun)
Streaming to green stones---

And of a pigeon cote:
              of
              a tarred roof, roofed with doves.

## QUEST(ION)
* * *


I've stayed
        myself ---stunted
        lines that were hatching:
Quietly stopped up both ears with wax
    So that I should never hear nor reveal
    My naked thoughts.


Thus words elude
        me, though I grasp at
        their sound with greed, intent
Upon capture ---can I
    Attain an intertwining of sense with voice
    To entertain


**SIGNIFICANCE?**

# REDUCTION


Describe the cells
   In detail -- giving rules
   by which their interdependencies
Can be controlled.

Mechanisms
   Are essential: dissect the
   Brain into bits of tissue --
Or better:

Knot the bits
   Into nets of predictable actions.
   Thus each act becomes
Sufficiently abstract

To be publishable --
   (And publication is the end
   to which I shatter movement
Into facts).

## CHEWING

The wheat grain contains
    itself--
Is creation in
   transition
   between
   being and
Beatitude.

Rice grains
   ripen instantly
Into exact replicas of
   infinitude,
   and affirm my
   intention
To exist.

Love for the moment of change from outer to
   inner touches incestuous desires--
Earth is the mother who
   feeds me
   completely
   as I go deeply
Into seed.

As I eat, I am
   eaten, yielding
Uniqueness
   as a sacrifice
   rising to the source
   of all my
Energies.

Each grinding movement is
   awareness that
Discrete beings
   blend into
   the flow from light
   to my momentary
Life.

**The sun**
   **becomes**
   (Rising)
   my own
   beating
**Blood.**

## NOTHING DOING

Write this poem. Listen! Is anything being said that means anything?
So much noise ---- where's the voice? I must be going deaf!

I remember having heard a voice of coruscating marvels! What luminosity of
words! That speaker must be dead (or perhaps, has merely gone on vacation).

Do I expect too much? Isn't the miracle of voice, of speech, of
hearing itself sufficient? Can I simply hear some word as **that word**?


(And *what* word?)


Listen to the cars whiz by. Listen to the sibilant computer. Hear ringing
keyboard clatter (today's cobblestone hooves). My inner voice hides.

This shows poetry "on demand" is not my strength. Can I write more often
---- bring up words, each time, that I will ever want to listen to again?

Or do I, dipping into this pool, strip it of all its
treasures? (Today's dip ---- nothing much found.)


So what's the *word*?

# PLUNGES DOWNWARDS

## I. TRYING TO PAINT

I look. I look at <u>this</u>. I look long.
Now I begin to see -- I can see this!
   Its subtlety is infinite. Where does seeing end?
   There is no end, except I chop my seeing short.
Complexity and uniqueness beyond imagining in this one scene.
Am I to attempt a representation? <u>This</u> truly brings me
                    to the terror of the situation!

For what can I show? If I were perfect draftsman
With skills honed over a lifetime, could I catch more than a miniscule hint
                of what I am seeing?
   With my sparse skills I can catch far less.
   Is it therefore vain to attempt an image?
I decide I will flail -- dip brush: experiment. My marks distract me
                from seeing.
Nevertheless -- I <u>will</u> create a pattern. Now my struggle has little
                to do with what I saw.

            *     *     *

I made this foolish image -- what does it tell me?
It reminds me that I looked; that (before) I saw; that I was speechless.

   The seen descended, gallery beyond gallery.
   God was evident right here -- this infinite progression of the seen:
                this bottomless possibility
                of seeing.

            *     *     *

Why do I not look more? My mind's awe and terror at disappearance
   Within the vast world it could never dream of holding
                is my barrier.

## II. SILENT VORTEX

Vision still
    eludes mind.

Stillness permits vision, seeing beyond mind.
    Mind says "I must mark that down!" and dies attempting.
    The still vision eludes all describing.  In seeing it all
I blow mind away.  Wonder then
illuminates soul.

               ---- Every container cracks open,
                    simultaneously.


Was life locked into a box?  Did streaming lights,
    blood-webs coagulate?  Was being fossilized?

Before the world was entered with the eye, mind
    knew all the answers.  But vision has shattered
    all that certainty: every answer, dying, is alive with million maggot
questions.  The structure of
self, therefore, writhes in agony.

               ---- (Do you say I should not be
                   tired?)

# GEMS

## I.

Gems reside within, but
I hide them
    from myself.
That which I <u>find</u>,
I want to <u>have</u>:
    it is
myself.

       (The little boy's explorations
were not approved: He should
    prepare himself
    to earn wages.
Rather, he explored each
    part of
himself.)

## II.

Child's curios were lost,
scattered, sunk in landfill. After years
    earning wages,
    something glinted.
Gems in junk. Old man,
    wondering, saw
sparkler!

Flash of terror. I can't
follow that flash: it tears
    status quo ante, it
    threatens dropping
off vertical glass wall into
    startling
disrepair.

### III.

Result: Delight? Despair? Or
dulling? Halt! I can smear the facets with
    tenacious films that will
    hide the flash --- return me to
my beliefs. Or: can simply close
    eyes, and
doze.

        (What's the night wage earned
    thus? Insignificant! Sun is
        beneath the earth, no
        light to reveal
flashing. Therefore
        I can
slumber.)

### IV.

    Repeat: flash
in garbage. Glint
    of unrequited
    puzzlement. That
glitter does not fade
    easily! I become
restless.

    Gems reside within, but
I hide them
    from myself.
    That which I find,
I want to have:
    it is
myself.

# THOUGHT ON THOUGHT

Invisibly, each
    being is
        architect, acrobat,
Prestidigitator.

What marvelous,
    unprecedent-
        ed contortions,
Performed with skill,

    Deceptive in rapidity
        as bird's
            song (too fast, so
Hardly known).

But these doings
    ordinarily
        delight no-one, as
They are so ordinary:

Ease deceives. (The facile
    miracle
        unnoticed,
Unremarked.)

## WILD


Unbroken horses run
    toward new forage,
mill, prance, living
    by horse laws.


These beauties will not
    work for me.  Harnesses,
unassembled, hang on
    walls, will remain


empty till the wild
    become tame.  Now
feed them, feel
    their energies.


Know their eyes and
    dispositions.
They are not yet
    ready to help.

## BOOKWRITING
### (trying to congeal mind's exploration
### into some fat, static block of paper)


### I.

Fishstew: complex flavors derived from living beings,
sacrificed. Single plangent bowl, melange of species

unified by flame, is what I want to serve. So I fished
this stream. Those mindforms were caught: beauties

that lay quivering in the crill are now on ice, waiting
for a new complement. But other essential lives, glimpsed,

flick the surface. Drop another hook, then watch
in silence. (Intently pull the next fighter in.)


### II.

Can my source stream onward, endlessly? No: rivers
flood, brooks die. The mindstream within which each

Question swims is fickle: Look, here the water backs
up, blocked by these great rocks. The trickle from

above, too slight to maintain flow, soaks into
dry bottom. Where did swimmers go? Do they

survive? More water is needed, and the channel must be
freed (recurrent chore for conserving natural resources).

### III.

What about the stew? Can mindstream be opened, sufficient
fish caught? Today it won't wash! Insights remain dammed,

circulation feeble. Promised emoluments contaminated
questioning. Water/work stinks! Inevitably, flow

blocked becomes mud: Look! Myriad bits, each still
glittering, are sunk to puddle's bottom, turning to

garbage! So work: shoulder against boulder, shove it. That
one also, till flow's opened, stream renewed. Then these

myriad bits do move -- drunken fragments dancing, sunlight
showing colors. Swimmers bob up, they shine! Catch one and

Sniff: That is fragrant! Perfect material for
stew. (Soon my range of kinds will be sufficient.)


### IV.

But for all that, there is still much to do. After all, fish
will not congeal to compose the desired dish easily. The chef

must fuss. Cooking the succulent melange is
arduous work. A flame must be sustained, for

Unity comes slowly. Disparate thoughts
mingle with reluctance.

      (Or dream of horses: heavy harness can't fall into place
      without careful construction of traces and frames.)

Author's Fantasy:
EXPECTING BOOKBIRTH
(Salute to the not-yet-emerged)


I.


This unborn volume
    calls me.
The uncreated speaks, demanding
    entrance to created life.

        Voice
            of (engendered)
            understanding
        will not be stilled -- its syllables
            hardly coherent, yet
            conveying (angelic)
        meanings, newly
            minted (the die
            not yet opened).  For

Structure
    grows of itself,
unfolds, transformation
    upon transformation

Wondrous hiddenness,
        branching forth as
pear tree, fruit still
        forming.


*127*

## II.

Carry the fetal
    book, feel its
kickings.  Prepare
    clean garments.


It <u>will</u> come out!


Forming:
    Great power, unsuspected --
      Chaos comes to form silently.
Generative forces,  unseen,
    knead and
      reknead the dough...


There is struggle,
    pangs (contractions?) --
      The outcome uncertain, yet
clearly foreknown.
    (What
      is visible?)...

## NATURAL HISTORY OF POETRY

### I.

    Enter my
**Museum**
    of sights and beings:

    Rooms display mindframes
        preserved from ancient epoches.  Look:

**That** specimen
    (its plumage carefully arranged)

    Glows with
        seeming life!

**Admire** it:  Then
    pass on to

    The next).

### II.

    Note: finch when
**Alive**
    flew between trees,

**Perched** (having escaped hunters),
    breath rapid, watchful.  Not

    To be caught
        is art.  Yet:

**Sleeper** fell,
    arrow-pierced, and

    Was mounted
        (so: did not

**Decay**).

III.

Elsewhere, zoologic
**Garden**
exhibits bodies extracted

Living from dismembered jungles
(remember: alien cultures

**Perished,**
with no obituaries).

Each catalogued item (present or
absent powers to move) can only

**Hint**
that other worlds

Existed.


IV.

Mourning and disclaimers,
However, grow
no fruit. Dear

**Friend**, Please
view my collections

Assembled

by careful
**Labor**. I wish to learn whether
these touch your

Life. To give
pleasure is my greatest

**Honor!**

# READING (HEARING) A POEM

--i--

What is the "ring" of it?  Is it
 Heart-song?  Does the

Reader (hearer) 'see'
 *Into* a surprising depth?

--ii--

Is the story endless, yet always
 Celebrating its ending?  (*Does it*

*Tell itself, rising to the lips with*
 *Each exhaled breath?*)

*131*

## THOSE WHO HAVE DANCED
(Stretchings, Burnings)

Homage to
five dancer friends

Those who have danced
Glow.
Dance illuminates time, as
What rhythm more
    complexly human
Exists?

*

Movement of self,
Displayed,
Explicates that which
Cannot be
    said. What
Supports

The inner turnings?
Dancer
Demonstrates elegant
Recreation by which
    mind is
Flesh:

Friend, I am watching --
Mime hosannahs of the
Heavenly host, I beg you! Yes --
Please pierce my comfort with
Mourner's agony. But more --
Know remorse, and send this
    arrow also.

Dance shoots straight, heart's
Pulse is reset.

*

Who does the
Dancer become?

Has archer's
    life
(Has being also the
    bow
From which arrows'
    impetus
Derived)

    Reformed every
    Inner tissue?

Stretch: encompass
    compassion.  Be
Receptive target
    (gossamer softness,
Following each thrust),
    conformable
To extreme actions.

    Can stretching transform
    Simple structures?


*


Example: How are vessels
    made?  Will
Flexible basketry
    perform
Functions of
    brittle
Jugs, and not break?

    Stretch, twist, contort
    to postpone fragmentation.

*133*

Once conformable clay
    hardens, the
Pot must not be
    dropped.
Yet ultimately,
    shattering
Happens.

    Shards will hold
    Nothing.


                *


Basket responds differently
    to a blow:
Fibers stretch, the
    force is
Widely distributed,
    impetus
Enters the whole.

    Structure deforms
    Without disruption.

If the weave
    holds, the
Contents are not yet
    lost:
Basket, accepting
    imposed motions,
Survives by
    yielding,
So does not dump its load now.

    Its danger, rather,
    Is from flames.

(The compassionate being
Will burn, not shatter.)

\*

Will this one crumble
    or burn?  Has discipline
    of dance remade
the vessel?

Was there an alchemical
    burning, that lost
    brittle substance,
leaving weave of fibers

(Transmuting
    mind as body, making
    mesh from which
hurled stones rebound)?

Transformed beings
    glitter without glaze --
    each vessel, porous,
weeping living water.

(Emergent inner fluid,
    wetting outer surface, reflects
    celestial
light.)

# HISTORY

## I.

Trace out (past)
    trajectory
    of mind.
Residues
    fade, yet
    remain:
(Scratched
    rock, bent
    twig, pebbles
Tumbled . . . what tiny
    story hides
    along the way?)

Almost nothing left;
    little sign of
    this walker!
Does any history
    of footpaths
    remain?  Yes:
Roads, enfolded only
    within one
    who walked,
Will die.  Yet each step
    taken supports
    present body.

II.


Thought, a flight of
        starlings; not
        each wing, or
Its feathers.  Rather,
        the pull of muscle
        at bone.  And
Wind worked against:
        multiple beats
        shine in
Mind.  Flock turning,
        dives; *swoop*
        resonates!

Awake to
        tumble of
        wings, I
Construct dance of
        changes.  High
        pattern
Pulls me to
        invent
        flight.
I know only (mind
        trembling) my one
        dance.


III.


Thus memory
        grows (only
        reforming
Forms), but
        returns . . .

## TIMELESS RESONANCE

for Jana


Voice of angels (here!)
    Held only for me. Where
        did Speech
Originate? Speaking
        recalls women and men
    Who lived since
Voice began.


Reading (now), I caress
    *Words*: Create each word
        lovingly. This
Gift *is* lives
        reborn --- instant
    Shout to honor
Ancestors.


                        (Just now, "<u>lift</u>!")


Say therefore (within)
    You *hear* myriad
        voices: Is
Each syllable
        only a chorus of
    This body's
Organs?


                Or can my pronunciations
                    Enliven songs sung
                        by those in
                Residence (eternally)
                        within
                    Those who
                *Hear*?

# 8.

## soundings
## and *ENDINGS*

## ELLIPSIS


I shall say soon "it is well
                    finished"
--------but cannot yet.


I still feel noon
                    undiminished
--------as grass shines wet


with rain that shuttered my window.


The wind
          that shook my door
                    took the storm
                    (and dries the rain)
          but will bring
More.

# WIND-OMENS

I find, rending on the sea
      a lea of butterflies
(Torn from the leaves of a shore-seeding tree)
         which swarm and scatter, tatters of a cloud
           that reforms (intact, tangled and muttering)
In myriad skittering branchlets.


Contrivances with mind, actors?
      or blown spray (littering -- blind
      -- the bark, resigned to being flung from rocks)?


Soon, flying flocks of leaves will lock the season;
      as my brain bows to greet such tattering --
      one by one, of its leaving cells:


The end, happening.

## MOMENT

Dreams reveal the soul:

The real bowl holds
      oil anointing torn leaves
      I feed upon.

Each mind transforms
      its matter. Water
Raised to drink is clear, refracting
      her I watch across
      the table. She swims over

And I drink /


We roll in green grass
      whole
      one between the two.
Heaven and earth are waiting as we reel
      (and know) and spin, holding
      a written command that
We won't read:

"I shall not stay forever."

(The scroll is hard to see
      I can't really see it
      I thought it was here

Someone else can write it again

The words are always the same --

"But who will love the world when I am gone?")

The role of lover is nothing:
      To love is to act.
      That which is loved is all

(And all in all). I shall be whole

For an instant longer.

## AFTER LEARNING OF ANOTHER ENDING --

Sorry about the
Swift shafts
Of light /
Pain

The HARROW cuts parallel lines into resilient, frangible soil,
filled with roots and myriad burrowing forms that hide
and proliferate.  The cutting is sweet and savage.
Each round blade slices plant and beast lives.
Yet they bear it.    The earth rejoices
to be opened.  (Room for new growth.)

I'll go now.
Gone to the reaper.
Always leaving, leaves turning toward the sun
then split to compost.  Other forms coming, who
eat my meat with gratitude, grow, become a fine
loamy humus that is eternal life.

All is forgiven,
in the end.
Life
is.

CLIMBING   (decline as ascent)


for Sam Atkin
(2 years before his death)


The treasure recedes forever.
The route, treacherous, grows more and more beautiful.
Pursuit excites.  What pleasures!  Fascination with the Way.
Knowledge of myriad particular solutions brings hope that the ultimate

Will be found.

Maintenance of the machines is of constant concern.
They work very well, and capture exquisite rewards.
Some, however, are proving less reliable than before.
Therefore new strategies, omitting them, are essential.

The old way cannot be trusted.

Reorganization of operating plans is the order of the day.
This however is very difficult since the attention of the experts
is almost entirely focussed on the absolute requirement for
More energy.  Yet it must be done.  All this takes a long time.

Clearly, the equation, though still soluble, grows more difficult.
Hillary suffered from reduced oxygen.  The need to carry essential
supplies up steep slopes undoubtedly limited his achievable height.
This struggle is analogous.  Yet the vista reached now

Has never been seen before.


*144*

### end-life as high-dive
(Father: origin and support)


[APPROACH]
Step up onto the board.
Then the slow walk
toward the tip, to try the spring.
a few testing bounces to get the rhythm of return.
Then back to the beginning.

[SUPPORT]
Board is strong. Pace forward again. Feel
hard resilience beneath feet (I am held up,
striding safe to the end). Jump: plunge
(energy of dropping will be returned).

[IMPETUS]
*This* is the moment of truth: Impelled upward,
Leave ground forever (supporter will not touch these soles again).
Thus enter time's last shining arc.

[DEPARTURE]
Dive: Exact flight downward, displaying
joy and terror (incarnate in my being here, in motion).

[FREE FALL]
Now: Choice of ultimate freedom, totally determined. Body will

Complete its path, aiming toward waves, water, the grave.
Swing *serious* (sing). Dropping happens (precisely) once.
**Here I am!**


- - - - - - - - - - - - - - - - - - -


[ANTICIPATION]
**This Being will enter water (will re-enter God's primordial ocean).**
Descent: Will it end? (Will it continue?

*Will I meet my father? Will I meet my God?*)


*145*

## SURVIVING SPOUSE

He left slowly, in no hurry.  All his movements weakened.
What could he carry?
    His body from the bed to the table?
    His food from his plate to his mouth?
Both! -- But with greatest difficulty.

The wife had to help.  The wife had to do.
The wife had to make.
    Always.

The wife and he had, earlier, travelled the world.
They laughed, looked, ran.  Had befriended
    salty characters with
    piercing minds
Everywhere.

He had made the dough, and had listened to everyone's troubles.
Then -- disease and age -- he was in
    bad trouble.

The wife worried, wanted to ease his way.  Always thinking of
him -- his wants, woes, ways.
    What blessing!
    All-consuming solicitude.
Forever?

No, he did not stay!  The wifely virtues have
no subject now.  The turn toward self is
    difficult!

Widowhood:  The whole split.  A vast emptiness.  The other nowhere!
All the myriad attachments
    torn, open, oozing...
    Silence in the night is
most difficult.

Where is the Demand?  Who needs the willing servant?  Where is that voice
that face, that mind, that life, that being, that prison, that task, that
    love?

The whole strong structure of life cracked -- then half
dropped off.  The part left grieves.  Widowhood sucks.
    Dryness.  Nurturance finally
    defeated.
Where is the way?

Who cares?  What's left?  Why go on?  Woebegone, without
hope of true renewal, because the center
    is gone, forever.  (Try to survive, however.
    What else is there
to do?)

## DISINTEGRATION OF BINDERS
### (Slowing, Sinking, Seeding)


Here I am. I await the grower.
The seed-drill sinks in. I slide
            into slick loam, and wait. The dark
            silence has become comfortable. Why
Am I here? Is the farmer even more patient
Than I am? Will I wait forever? Will I grow?

                    *    *    *


Watered structure dissolves (rock to gel, to colloid --
Tight bonds cut
        by pain-energy permit
        the flowering of
soul). Here's the chance, as all happening enters, for my being
To knit itself differently than before.

                Can such liberation require ending?
                The first veil of heaven is world's
                        universal sadness,
                        through which
                immortal youth refused to look.
                Look! -- Chinks appear, a new shining!

I'm stopped. Wait here. Watch my fundamental
withering. Porosity comes with age.
        Gaps: The smooth surface
        wrinkles, tears -- deteriorates.
When young, all held together seamlessly
(so swarming pain-energies would not penetrate.)

                    *    *    *


                Now everything opens: The mesh spreads, life-texture
                unravels, and thereby the living force, though
                        weakened, nevertheless
                        is finally unbound.
                Dispersion of losses, confluence of imperfections
                Is my great opportunity! I enjoy this startling digestion.

## MEDITATION (travelling home)


I stay here.
   Another turbulent year
   Over and why not!

Here harmonic variants vibrate:

Life's long and taut string, plucked
   Once, gradually quieting. The crescendo
   Was near the start (and harsh).

Diminuendo followed, a slow dying of discord.
   The fundamental becomes more clear, as it dies
   (A pure tone -- a prayer).

      The tone prays
      The song remains --
      Its diminishment imperceptible.

Each moment provides its own dimension. The force here now
   Is all I have, and is
   Exactly what I need.

## To(know) ?
======

How can I tell
    where I am?
Is this the world
    of order?
(Or of
    disorder?)


        That which I would see
            I cannot.
        But most difficult: What
            is the seeing? What is
        Seeing? Am I seen?
            What sees? (Who? -- )


            How have I gone about this business?
                By travelling to the lakeside:
        I lie down, listen.  Soft splash says
                some fish flicks the surface.
        But can I see it?  Why bother -- I know
                it's there.  (It's swimming...)


Who comes
        to this place?
How does the comer
        arrive?
(From what place comes
        the comer?)


        This observer
            is never observed.
        Looker
            not seen?
        (Just
            looking -- )


        Weed-seed dropped,
            disappeared.
        No more wind, nor light
            here.
        (Yet something
            is happening...)

# BREAKINGS

## I. State

This is the place. (Can I render myself fluid?)
    The flowing stream can enter all crevices, so long as
        the direction is downward.
      **Deepening** is natural! Fluid enters the rock, fills
infinitesimal cracks.
When the freeze comes, the rock will be

Broken.
    Can I drop
      through minute cracks of my hard mind? It is
      minding, guarding its polished surface.    Look: The rock glitters,
      reflection
      astounds me. --
  I will go no lower:
      I am supported by hardness.
      It is my salvation. (To flow is to die.)

        ^^^^^^^^^^^^^^^^^


## II. Another State

Running water seeks its own level. (Freezing water cracks its vessel.)
    Spring melting brings fluidity. Seek out
      the cracks! All sinks.
    **All becomes** part of the calm surface -- the flat
      of minimum energy: in that calm
Interface I see my own

Reflection.
    Careful -- the cliff has
      cracked. Watch the
      sliding! Rock slides down the icy slope.
    An arrogant movement toward a
      lower level. Will it
      splash? --
    This is dangerous:
      The lagoon's smooth top will be broken for an instant.
      The rock will sink to the bottom, there to be supported by

Older rock. Watch: it is
happening. (It is done.)

        ^^^^^^^^^^^^^^^^^

# RETURN

Who knows the way up the mountain?

I started at the top, but lost my way.
Being born was precipitous.
Recovering the place is a lifetime's exploration...

      *      *      *

The ascent continues forever
Return is step and step

      Return to a place where I never was
          (yet I was there)
      Return to a time that stretches ahead, invisible
          (it's just begun)

How will I know that I have arrived (I'm afraid
    there will be no-one to ask)
When did I start the climb (the sun
    is already low)
      My father told me there will be a roof, to protect me
          from rain
      (The place is now being built, brick by brick)
      My mother told me of a hearth, to keep me
          warm
      (The wood is still growing; I will cut and split it)

The end is hidden
**The beginning got lost . . .**

# AGE...

* * *

Do hard places
  dissolve
  gradually?

Does wisdom
  sneak past the
  guard posts?

Can I slide into
  solemnity with a
  mirthful countenance?

Is the fruit already
  sweet -- firm though
  about to drop?

How long must I
  hang on, as ripening
  continues?

When the stem
  parts, what
  then?

Is the receiver
  a soft loam, where
  new trees arise?

* * *

I suspect this story
  has a happy ending.
New trees are
  much needed.

## TRAIN NYSTAGMUS

(Is each
      night
      a saccade?)
(Is each
      day
      a pursuit?)


Train swiftly carries me
      toward another
            station.  Here I
Observe
      out the window.  Light
            reveals myriad

Objects.  What beautiful
Landscapes!  The constant
            change
Confounds me.  I tremble,
Amazed!

This scene
      does not repeat (as
            sunny fields
Zoom by.)  This ride is
      forever new.  The
            rider tries to

**Understand.**


                  (Every night,
                        another saccade.)
                  (Every day,
                        another pursuit.)

## LIFE'S ESSENTIAL FRAMEWORK IN
## RECIPROCAL CONTAINMENT --


Nestings of
Generations are
Miraculous!

Each emergent being
        falls into its nest:  Each young
Generation unfolds within
        the older.
This is obvious.  It is outer truth.

Within, each young generation carries
        the older.
All nested, generation
        within generation, back
To the beginning.

Two infinite series of nested nestings,
        each series contained within the
Other:  In fact each whole series
        infolded within every
Level of the forward
        and rearward series...

How astonishing!  (Such obvious
Miracles may themselves be
Myriad, yet remain unseen.)

# REVERBERANCE

### 1.

Take clay and water.  Mold mud.
Bricks, fitted to mind's form
Form a cavernous space, vented.

Cut and split oak, load this new
Oven, kindle a flame.
Fire

Suffuses the hidden retreat.
All within grows
Luminous.

Regulate the fire's
Breathing, to make
Charcoal.

### 2.

Clay, water, mud, bricks -- the second oven.
Take ore, charcoal, fire: make
Brass.

Beat the brass to thin sheet,
Shape it.  It will become a
Wide

Bowl.  Make oak frame from which to
Hang the bowl.  Hang it with two strings, and
Gaze

Upon it:  It is
New!  What can it
Say?

3.

Wind cotton about an end of rod.  Then
Swing it.  Struck, the wide bowl
Sounds.

The meaning of the making is now
Revealed.  Gong shakes my
Being.


4.

That sequence, just read,
Exemplified what this
Poem is, in
Itself.

As it is read, the
Reader (so writer intends),
Makes

A gong, which, at
Terminus, is
Struck.


5.

Three questions for
The end:

Did my life begin in clay and fire, molding
Matter -- do I become wide reverberant
Bowl?

Will a great vibration be
Reason for
All?

Is this gong (myself) being
Readied for a final
Blow?

I will not answer... (But
Know.)

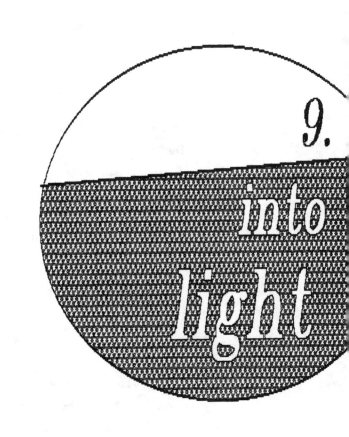

9.

into
light

# NIGHT SEEKERS

------------------------

The queer fowl
　　luminesce
　　in darkness.


　　　\/　　\/


Our river, rounding its chunked stones, has
Ducks
　　who paddle among the stems,
Rasp "What? What? What?"
　　(grasping not much) and dip
　　heads under the fleeting
Surface.　　**No sign yet.**
　　Wait.


　　　\/　　\/


A haze of moonlight
　　hints at their moving, white
　　through shaken grass.

# Honoring Lillian

How did she teach us?
To JOIN EVERYTHING TOGETHER.
The inner working is hard to know. I sense it sometimes, with
concentration.
Close attention MUST be paid! Does heaven feel the rain
interpenetrating?
Does the earth it soaks know heaven?

Hear me, O ye grasses.
Be still, and listen!
The message is so small, the ant dwarfs it, and passes it by.
I have, in fact, never seen it. I sense it within, sometimes.
        I will stay here, and listen with you.

            Ah --
if only I could stay!
I would become rich as a dog in a boneyard.
            However
I *never* stay! Isn't it amazing!
I'm a flying monkey, stealing Joseph's many-colored coat
            -- and Long Gone.

Please don't forget, I beg you,
to water my plants when I'm gone.
They dry out, and cry for water.
(*They* had a message for me, but I couldn't hear it.)

Remember.

        Please watch.
            Watch with me! Isn't the tracery of light shining
            to the bottom through the ripply surface
            beautiful?
            How can we leave now? The day starts with watching these
            ripples.

# NOTHING, BEATING...

Nothing seen
   (The flash of
      darkness)

Nothing heard
   (The substance of
      silence)

Nothing felt
   (The stroke of
      emptiness)

Slide along the page
Dissolve
Leave me in peace

   Depth past understanding
   Bottom of heaven
   Hollow hiding heart.

Water of life streams
   underfoot as
I leap from stone to stone.

There is no stopping my pulse,
   my pulse, my pride, my proposing
until I die.

*invisibility of the trunk*
*inconceivability of the roots*

- = < ( [ | \ / | / \ | ] ) > = -


Leaves glitter, glisten,
        twitter, flirt, jitter.
Each fully individual.
Unutterable separation --
The outermost reaches of differentiation:
Each alone / All outside / Exquisitely separate.

        (All
        Alone -- not
                        all one; rather
        One infini-
        tesimal.)

        -=<|>=-

Stay.  Gaze:
        Leaf-stem is detectable! --
        note the subtle connection
        to unseen branchlet.
        (Watch all the leaves: their motions
                betray convergent connections.)

Now:
        My sight apprehends
        each hidden branchlet
        through linked shudders of leaves.
        (Thus I abstract the swaying support
        I cannot see.)

Then each branchlet must converge
                (to its indescribable branch).
And clearly all the inferred branches
        form a structure -- a
        stupendous unity (leading
        *together* and *down* ...
More I cannot know.)

        **Trunk**
        **beyond conceiving**
                        **supports the visible world**
        (fluttering in infinite
        separations).


*161*

Only where
  an inner mesh is reweaving
Itself
Can there be
  Consciousness.

The weave of wondering!  There must be
Some kind of
  Wonder.  Without surprise -- anticipation of crashing --
All my alertness lapses into
  Snores.

How can the mechanism
  remain open to
Rebirth?
Each instant requires
  Couplings.

Mind's life is not only machine.  Every fixed
Rhythm has infinite
  Underbeats.  Brain cannot be contained by our images.
  Neuronal fecundity creates generations of creation, in an
  Instant.

Therefore:  This plant continually
  generates non-random
Newness!
Nothing else under my life
  Can.

## MUSIC

Those sounds
    recalling pulsed blood
Shatter constancy: Levelness
    disappears -- all becomes up-down.

Even seeing trees
    changes -- their shudders were
Random: But heart's beat is
    there too (my blood, shaking leaves!)

This won't do. Music
    introduces spurts of
Compassion to the scene: Melodic
    cries, shouting -- "Life cannot stop!"

        *       *       *

What perfect construction! The bones
    of this body articulate with miraculous
Bravado: No movement was ever more
    precise, yet so lacking in finality.

Therefore I continue to follow
    a swinging, a rising stroke. I listen without
End, and the stroke does not stop -- it
    transforms itself to one instant, eternal.

        *       *       *

Earth's continuance is now promised, and
    life's pulsations guaranteed; strange
Lights, offered to God, were
    not acceptable (but music was!)

End in beginning, change without
    difference. Sacrifice with
Nothing given away. Is this not a
    miracle? All paradox resides in the present note.

## LOOKING OUT

What's up?

    Climb.  Reach the
        top.  See another
    Mountain.  And: As
        departings, so
    Arrivings.

Can I ever
Unfold all
Infoldings?

No.  Each one, unfolded
Shows another
Within.

    Behind every
        unravelling, are
    Threads beyond number.  This fact
        overpowers reason.
    So why go on?

That's life!

## MICROCOSM: WHO MINDS?

**Each interior ramifies infinitely**

Fractal hallways bend into infinitesimal
    convolutions;
Each pathway passes from any point back
    to itself
Over a route that covers each world,
    ages past, all time to come.

Finite routes extend without end,
    passing every far-off place.
Such complexity does not yield to
    consecutive analysis.
Even asymptotic approximation is
    no help, simplification no savior.

Paths so fine seem fragile --
    but numerosity gives strength:
How?  Does redundancy beyond imagining
    produce mind?  No:
Mind emerges from myriad elements with
    zero redundancy.

Milliard paths the same, yet none
    alike!  Similarity is illusion -- The
Real is totally without similitude.

Thus every road, confluence beyond conceiving,
    provides difference everywhere.  That is the way
God is One!  The Infinite Path is everywhere unique.

## RECITATION

Gong, once crafted, can be
Kept, ready to be
Lifted from its case,

Rehung.  Hear those
Clashes!  Now (as I
Speak,

Each word
Resonant) another
Stroke.

What glory!  Poem grows
Infinite progression: World generated,
Fades.

(Is my life
One word?)

# SEPARATED LIGHT

## I.

Unlink fire from the ember
Separate coal from glow
It can't be done
Yet must, because
Chilled rooms await flame.

Take the coal, then: generate
Gas. This will burn
Elsewhere, and
Later. Burning
Removed from the coal.

Wholes can be
Separated. Knowledge
Of separations does not
Come easily. Hard knocks
Teach distance.

But the result is amazing!
Fire removed from coal
Gathers power -- it can do
More: its heat has left the
Body (which still vibrates)

* * *

I ask endless separations as
Way to come into a single
Flame: What better source of
    Light than myriad incandescent
    Molecules of the mantle? Each
    Alone in radiance.

Thus I remain luminous,
Wondering on illuminations
From other condensed beings.
    We all cohere, burning
    Separately (yet without
    Separation).

## II.

Take away congruences
(Loosen adherent tensions):
This route contradicts
Some wisdom, yet finds
Harmony through unbindings.

Coherent luminosities
Are possible when
States relax
(Uncoupled yet resonant),
Driven hard together.

What drives? This question
Troubles many sleeps. Its
Answer echoes wordless:
Another light allows
Agitation to release light.

Listen to another song:
Each song echoes what had been
Sung. Lights of singers
No longer visible. How
Does that vibration endure?

*   *   *

Shall I remain luminous?
What supports kindlings
Upon other condensed beings?
     Miracle that we all burn
     Apart, yet cannot be
     Separated!

So: Seek endless separations as
Way to come into single
Flame. Enter now this source of
     Light: The myriad incandescent
     Molecules of the mantle -- each
     Alone in radiance.

# AFTERWARD

## The Name

Why "Alarms and Mirrors"? I write sometimes to wake myself up. Can I awaken at least a little in this tiny moment, to know (some iota bettter) *where* and *who* I am? This enterprise is reflective -- mind reflecting its image as knower. (Yet how can mind observe its own vision?)

So for me the title is evocative. It speaks of *functions*, in shorthand.

What of the book's structure?

## The Plan

After having elaborated the plan for the book I looked again at the sequence of sections and noticed an interesting progression and symmetry that I had not seen clearly before. I had felt a need for each of the sections; I had set each up for poems of a certain thrust, with a certain range of intention.

When I had made a section for each perceived subgroup of the poems I had assembled, found I had nine sections. And I had placed them in an interesting progression: The first was for entering a way of seeing, for getting a first taste of a mind; the second for seeing concerns with world's hopes for continuance; the third for feeling one's relations with oneself and another; the fourth for mourning the dead; the fifth for despair, plunging down, and clowning; the sixth for holiday celebrations; the seventh for ways of finding the new form; the eighth for depths that had to do with destinations; and the ninth and last, lifting toward new lights of understanding.

I had made this structure with no clear vision or intention of symmetry, yet was astonished when I later examined it more closely. Looking at the whole form, I saw the middle part (**five**) as a deep drop ("the pits") dividing a beginning from an end. I then asked: Is the first half a movement toward finishing something old? Is the last half a movement toward beginning something new?

## Concentric Symmetry

I found more. I looked and asked -- do the forms pivot in some way about that 'drop' at the middle? Are there symmetries? What are they?

Here is what I saw:

All seems balanced about that "DOWNBEAT" center (**five**).

-- *sorrowful, contractive* celebrations (**four**:
"remember our sleepers") balanced against *joyous,
expansive* celebrations (**six**: "special occasions");
-- *social connection* (**three**: "myself / to another one")
balanced with *creative unfolding* (**seven**: "making
/ maker");
-- *ethical concern* (**two**: "for hope, love, and charity")
balanced with *purpose and finality* (**eight**:
"soundings and endings");
-- *blossoming intensity of this moment's prize* (**one**:
"this moment when...") balanced with *pointings
toward infinite vistas* (**nine**: "into light").

It's like this:

```
.   .   .   .   .   .   .   .   .   .   .   .   .   .   .   .   .   .   .
                             |
       (1) ◄─────────────────┼─────────────────► (9)
     Intensities             |            Opening of
     of the moment           |            infinities...
                             |
                             |
         (2) ◄───────────────┼───────────► (8)
       Good &                |            Purpose &
       evil                  |            finality...
                             |
                             |
            (3) ◄────────────┼──────► (7)
         Connection          |      Creation...
                             |
                             |
                 (4) ◄───────┼──► (6)
             Sorrow &        |  Joy &
             contraction     |  expansion...
                             |
                             :

                       (5)
                Accepting my reality's
                fragmentation...

.   .   .   .   .   .   .   .   .   .   .   .   .   .   .   .   .   .   .
```

This is very interesting. Everything was in place at the time I first saw these symmetries. (Thus, it had all been "intuitive", genrated by creative energies beyond my ordinary awareness and control -- as in most of the writing of each poem.) Observing this concentric structure now -- "after the fact" -- is a blast! It's a whole new unexpected, unanticipated exploration (as was each poem). Now I'm trying to "see what I said", in this new arena -- on this larger scale.

But it's still in part an abstract construction -- a glimpsed larger pattern: I don't yet know how well the individual poems will prove to fit with it. I'll see...

## Depths and Journeys

Is this a journey? Or is this a design for depths present or attainable in each moment? I'm sure it is <u>both</u>!

Think of the journey: Where does it take me? Does the journey go deeper and deeper -- the plunge to a pain-evoking depth. Go within, begin to see -- entrancement yet revulsion at any vision of one's mechanisms. Plunge. Hit bottom. Rebound with changed structure.

What about the 'depth'? How do I 'hit bottom'? Where does the 'rebound' begin? This place is suggested by the middle section of the book:

The transition (**five**), perhaps a 'bottom', or an *'outside'*, is *seeing* fragmentations and *accepting* them: -- is it dropping to a depth that is empty? Is it fragmenting the 'real', attaining a vapid superficiality, trivializing depths? Yet the *seeing* of this emptiness, of this triviality, brings awareness of something else beyond -- a <u>question</u>. And this question banishes unreflective sureness that visible realities are the ultimates.

*171*

## Going Deeper

This journey is not a single sequence in time. The journey is made again and again -- can be undertaken in every moment. That is the import of how these poems were written, and how the book-sections were then derived. Poems that later fitted all (or nearly all) of the nine sections were written in some of the earlier years, and in most years in the last decade. Thus I have been engaged in all stages of this journey for many years -- perhaps from the beginning.

What depths are potentially present in each moment? Can I set forth some design by which they might be attained? Does deepening require a plunge? (Does it require letting go, dropping down -- and then finally floating up?)

The "plunge" has to do with opening. Can one open to the myriad ordinarily rejected sights, scenes, scents, sensations? My usual place is to remain calm by *not seeing* that of which I disapprove; I throw it out totally -- but out from my awareness, not out from my existence, not out from my being. This is the prime mistake! (It is a version of the "repression" of which Freudians speak.)

Can I see the deep truths and *accept* them? I *must* accept them, because they are there! Yet I do not: All kinds of confusion, twistedness, untruth, loneliness and alienation follow from this misguided act of mind.

How do I first approach the depth? Do the sections of the first half suggest how? I approach the depth by attending to nearer amazements, and watching them as steadily as I can (sections **one**: "this moment when..." and **two**: "for hope, love, and charity"). Such attention attracts the deeper truths, which by sympathy with the amazements I accept, become also more acceptable. This effort is valuable. It "*works*"!

A second approach is to attend deeply to the plight of other beings -- then I know my own is not unique, and therefore not so despicable. I see *their* struggle, and can more easily accept and continue with my own. (Sect. **three**: "myself / to another one".)

A third approach is to delve deeply into the reality of mortality -- that of all family and friends I know, and by reflection my own. This sets a frame within which my disapprovals seem picayune. How can I not love it all, when it will be over so soon? (Sect. **four**: "remember our sleepers".)

## Another Journey: Going Out from Center, and Returning

But may the journey be also seen as beginning in the opposite direction -- is this "center" toward which I drop not a most peripheral of externalities?   Do I travel up, outward to the surface, the "outside" -- then back down to depths? (This is the image of the concentric structure turned inside out, with level five as the globe's surface.)  Seen so, I journey *starting* from a center (one), going out to ends of earth, to unbounded fragmentations, to immersion in mechanicalities (five) -- which however now are seen. Then back to a new center... -- the same place, known now for the first time (Eliot).

. . .

Yet here the first image still fits, after all. The drop feels to be a reflective return, as I come successively to each level, and finally to an inner opening, or "shattering" (the middle: sect. five); then later, on the far side of 'opening', come back to those levels again, but in a different way.  Here is how I begin to perceive each first-time touching of a level ("Nearside", on the way to but before the opening-'DOWNBEAT'-transition), and then each return to that level after the opening ("Farside"):

Nearside (**one**): Wanting to look, wanting to understand; finding glimpses of a *center*. Farside (**nine**): Knowing that/how ultimates are beyond seeing, are beyond understanding; finding a *way*.

Nearside (**two**): Dangers and beauties of the vast world; threat of an end; knowledge of good and evil (Tree of Knowledge). Farside (**eight**): Wonderment and finitudes of this being's existence; promise of an end; knowledge of the limits of understanding (Tree of Life).

Nearside (**three**): Opening to another being; coming together. Farside (**seven**): opening to other levels/ways of being; exploring paradoxes of how the maker is made.

Nearside (**four**):  Entering mysteries; grieving finalities. Farside (**six**):  Expressing wonderments; celebrating flowerings.

The sequence goes like this:

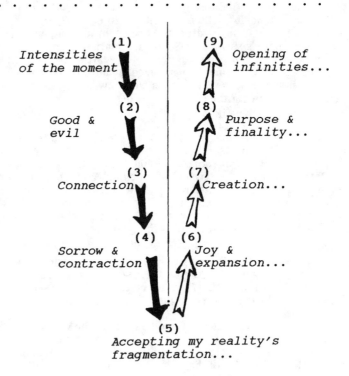

This vision of the whole book's structure, of its meaning, is that of cyclical process -- or better, of a patterning of movements that generate small transformations, each an "event" (Heschel's concept) -- that fundamentally alters one's apprehension of life. In this work, seeming disharmonies are fuel for fusing.

# DROP-SLIDE-STOP!

### 1

This day (this seed) opens as I remain
waiting, no patience, no impatience,
empty of all pushings, yet
pushed by that which knows no restraint.

### 2

This body simply resides, silent, resounding.
    Hear: Soundings reveal bottom beneath all waters, yet
beneath that bottom are echoes of deeper flows. Strata
streamed with lava: hard liquid of ancient probes.

### 3

    Soul's motion now seeks
cracks. This body --
liquid, yet brittle: ice
fractured everywhere.

### 4

Hold: Stay at one point, and that point
opens, unfolds. Each iota becomes
ocean, quietude, source (of
riches, of infinite emptiness).

5

Then: reversal. Nothing cracks
through. Openings close fast, before
entrance. Body, congealed, will not
bend (constrictions everywhere).


6

Solitude recoils, <u>seething</u>
begins. With great
patience, lover, I forget (to
wait.)


7

Therefore: <u>Close</u> that circle. (Can
center become circumference? Only if
circumference contracts.) Seeming
reversals conceal another opening.


8

Yet infinite unfoldings can only
continue. Every death is entrance, and
vica versa. Each moment I have
forgotten where I am.


9

Watch: This pulse, always the same,
never repeats. Each instant,
living blood reforms (thus
eternity overfloods) -- <u>remember</u>?


(1990)